August
Farewell

The Last Sixteen Days of
a Thirty-Three-Year Romance

To Christine

Wonderful to meet you
and thanks for all
your assistance at
Camp Widow Canada!

David

Toronto
Sept 2014

Also by David G. Hallman

Caring for Creation

AIDS: Confronting the Challenge

A Place in Creation:
Ecological Visions in Science, Religion, and Economics

Ecotheology: Voices from South and North

Spiritual Values for Earth Community

August Farewell

The Last Sixteen Days of
a Thirty-Three-Year Romance

David G. Hallman

iUniverse, Inc.
Bloomington

August Farewell
The Last Sixteen Days of a Thirty-Three-Year Romance

iUniverse books may be ordered through booksellers or by contacting:

iUniverse
1663 Liberty Drive
Bloomington, IN 47403
www.iuniverse.com
1-800-Authors (1-800-288-4677)

Because of the dynamic nature of the Internet, any web addresses or links contained in this book may have changed since publication and may no longer be valid. The views expressed in this work are solely those of the author and do not necessarily reflect the views of the publisher, and the publisher hereby disclaims any responsibility for them.

Any people depicted in stock imagery provided by Thinkstock are models, and such images are being used for illustrative purposes only.

Certain stock imagery © Thinkstock.

Cover author photo: The United Church of Canada

ISBN: 978-1-4502-8636-7 (sc)
ISBN: 978-1-4502-8638-1 (dj)
ISBN: 978-1-4502-8637-4 (ebk)

Printed in the United States of America

iUniverse rev. date: 01/20/2011

For Billy-boy, with love

Contents

Preface. ix
Acknowledgments xi
Chapter One—Friday, August 7 1
Chapter Two—Saturday, August 8 26
Chapter Three—Sunday, August 9 32
Chapter Four—Monday, August 10 37
Chapter Five—Tuesday, August 11 46
Chapter Six—Wednesday, August 12 52
Chapter Seven—Thursday, August 13 59
Chapter Eight—Friday, August 14 67
Chapter Nine—Saturday, August 15 75
Chapter Ten—Sunday, August 16 82
Chapter Eleven – Monday, August 17 88
Chapter Twelve—Tuesday, August 18 96
Chapter Thirteen—Wednesday, August 19 103
Chapter Fourteen—Thursday, August 20 110
Chapter Fifteen—Friday, August 21 118
Chapter Sixteen—Saturday, August 22 122
Chapter Seventeen—Sunday, August 23 130
Epilogue 141
  Photo Album 141
  August 23—Final E-mail Update 155
  September 1—Early Christmas Party Invitation 156
  September 13—Memorial Service. 157
  -   Service outline. 157
  -   Theological reflection—*Thank God for Good Friends* . 159
  -   Obituary 162
  -   Appreciations 163
  -   Recorded music—favourites of Bill and David 164
  November 23—Interment Service—*Good-bye, My Love* . . 166

Preface

August Farewell is the story of the sixteen days in August 2009 between Friday the seventh when my partner Bill was diagnosed with pancreatic cancer and Sunday the twenty-third when he died. Interspersed among the scenes of those days are vignettes drawn from our thirty-three years together as a couple.

I wrote this memoir primarily for myself. The experience of those two weeks was so intense, profound, and spiritual that I wanted to record it while it was still fresh, fearing that as I began forgetting details, it would feel as if I were losing Bill all over again.

Bill's process of dying was not something distinct from the rest of my life with him but rather the culmination. I hold those August 2009 memories in my heart by placing them in the context of a myriad of other life experiences that we had together from when we first met in August 1976. *August Farewell* is like a personal photo album for me, precious memories in words.

Bill and I did not live those two weeks in isolation. Friends and family accompanied us in person and in spirit, surrounding us in love. I am forever grateful to them.

Many who have read *August Farewell* report to me that they shed tears of their own at some points and laughed at other points. Most of all, they experienced it as a love story. They have encouraged me to share it more widely, suggesting it could be useful for people struggling with issues of identity, building a relationship, facing death (be it one's own or that of a loved one), or coping with palliative care in the final stages.

I have been humbled by readers' responses and the subsequent conversations have enriched my life. It is as if Bill keeps on giving me gifts.

He was always so generous in life. Why should now be any different?

David G. Hallman
Toronto, Canada
December 2010

Acknowledgments

I am deeply grateful:

- To the many friends, family, and Verve community members who supported Bill and me in his dying days and who continue to care for me during my ongoing mourning.

- To those who encouraged me to consider the sharing of *August Farewell* with a broader audience and helped me think through the issues involved, in particular, Marion Conklin-Griffith, Diane Hallman, Joan Burton, Janet Stemerdink, Denny Young, Doug O'Neill, Alanna Mitchell, Deborah Sinclair, Lee MacDougall, Tim French, Bill Aitchison, Allan Wilbee, Susan Wiseman, Gail Czukar, Ed Bennett, Laurice Mahli, Tamara and Dominic Glazier-Pariselli, Doug Dent, Barbara Young, Jay Lesiger, and Michael Cobb.

- To Dr. John Goodhew and Dr. David Robertson for their professional and personal support.

- To Joseph Luk and Craig Hanna for their creative contribution to the book cover.

- To the staff at iUniverse for their efficiency and sensitivity in bringing the publication of *August Farewell* to fruition.

Chapter One—Friday, August 7

"Are you awake?"

I groggily pry open my eyes. Bill is propped up on his elbow staring at me. He looks like he has been waiting for me to stir.

"Um, yeah I think so. What's up?"

"Now that you've had a few hours of sleep, there's something I need to tell you."

His voice is remarkably strong for 5:00 a.m.

"My doctor called last night and says that I should go to the hospital for some new tests."

Now I am awake. I had gotten home to our Toronto condo about midnight after a quick trip to our house in Stratford. Bill had been in bed asleep when I got in.

"What do you mean?" Maybe I'm not so awake. The words were clear, the significance less so.

"He's concerned about the results that came in from last week's ultrasound and blood work."

We'd been through endless testing over the past few months. Sorry, not we: *he*. I was just the chauffer. No, that's not right either. I had been the accompanier, the personal support system, and the primary caregiver, one of whose roles was to take him to the labs when his doctor ordered a new set of tests.

Each time we had gone back to his doctor for the results from these tests, we had different reactions. He was generally reassured because nothing serious had shown up. I was generally distressed because nothing serious had shown up.

There was something serious going on. I was convinced. And I wanted to know what.

Bill had lost fifty pounds since January. He was immensely proud of that because he had been trying to lose weight for years. Now the pounds were vaporising. He was convinced that he had discovered the best diet ever. Just eat half of what is on your plate. He became very enthused about his system and tried to encourage others to adopt it. For a while I objected that the weight was coming off too quickly to be healthy. I shut up after he repeatedly chastised me for raining on his parade.

The weight was the least of it though. Fatigue and pain were the biggies. He had so little energy that he was in bed most of the time. Though stoic about the pain, you could see the agony on his face. He would often get up during the night unable to sleep because of the discomfort. One night, I came out to the living room to discover him lying on the sofa, his body curled up against the pillows, one leg draped over the edge, and one arm up over the back. What looked like the most awkward of positions had been the best way he could find to mitigate the pain.

With all of this getting worse week after week, I wanted answers. The test results kept coming back showing little askew except for what they called a spasming oesophagus. That seemed a partial answer and he was given some medication that was supposed to help. He had been on it for weeks, yet things were still getting worse.

But now something had shown up in last week's ultrasound and blood work.

"He says that we should go to the emergency department as soon as possible. He's left a copy of the test results in an envelope taped to his office door. We can pick them up on the way."

"Okay, let's get going."

Anticipating that we had a long day ahead of us, we both showered and shaved. By the time he was ready, I had the wheelchair set up at the front door. For three or four weeks now, any time we went out, it was with the chair. He had surprised me by how little resistance he put up when I had suggested that it might be an idea to rent one. We quickly settled into a routine using it. Not that we were going out very much. Mainly just to the doctor's and to labs.

Thirty years ago, we didn't need to rent a wheelchair. We owned one.

When we first met, fell in love, and started living together, Bill was athletic and energetic, and was regularly out on the rink playing hockey with his buddies. Within six months of our meeting, his mobility became limited and he would tire quickly. He was diagnosed as having multiple sclerosis (MS). We often had to use the wheelchair when we went out.

That was a rough adjustment for him. No longer skating on the rink, he was now watching from the sidelines.

But he decided that he wasn't going to spend the rest of his life in a wheelchair. He didn't like the support groups that had been offered to him as a newly diagnosed MS patient. He found them depressing. He resisted the experimental drugs that the doctors proposed. He had always been disciplined about eating well and rarely took medication. He wasn't about to start, especially when they couldn't assure him of the efficacy of the drugs and when the list of side effects filled half the information sheet.

He pushed himself very hard. He struggled to get around without the chair, sitting down and resting frequently. His only compromise was to use a cane sometimes to reduce the risk of falling and injuring himself.

He would limit going out to times when he had had a chance to rest beforehand.

As a result, when people saw him, it was on one of those days when he was strong enough to be out and about. He looked fine. Lots of people who knew him casually had no idea that he had MS. They didn't realise that he was in bed much of the time. They just encountered him on one of his good days.

MS affects people in very individual ways. His was of a variety that, with sufficient rest, he was able to mask.

The deterioration, though slow, was inexorable. Every few years, he would have to reduce the number of music students that he was teaching. At his peak, he taught five days a week and had about thirty students. By the spring of 2009, he only had the stamina for one afternoon a week and six students.

Don't be locked. Please, please don't be locked.

As we pull up beside the mall entrance where Bill's doctor's office is located, I pray that we can get access to that envelope apparently taped on his office door with the copies of the aberrant test results. It is only 6:00 a.m. and I think it not unlikely that the place will be shuttered up tight against night vandals.

I'm out of the car in a flash, and as I approach the door, my heart sinks when I see the dead bolt securing the double door. I pull the handle anyway and am surprised by the amount of give. The two doors are indeed locked together but there is no bolt affixing them to the floor or ceiling so I am in fact able to pry the doors open quite easily. There is a God.

Once back in the car, we take a quick perusal of the reports. The blood work numbers don't mean anything to us except to note the capital *A* signifying abnormal. The ultrasound report concludes with a narrative description. "There is a marked presence of ascites in the peritoneal cavity that was not apparent on the previous ultrasound in late May." Neither of us has any idea what *ascites* is, but we are not in the dark for long.

We are at Toronto East General Hospital by about 6:30 a.m. Fortunately, the previous night's various crises have petered out and today's have not yet commenced, so the emergency department is remarkably placid. We're interviewed quickly by the triage receptionist, who is the only person that we are to encounter all day who seems slightly annoyed and perplexed about why we are presenting ourselves. She gives us a number and motions us to the waiting room. As I wheel Bill to the designated area, he spots an empty gurney parked along the corridor and directs me to it. These days, he's anxious to avail himself of any opportunity to lie down.

After what seems an interminable wait—though actually a relatively short time by most people's experiences in emergency departments—we are ushered into a room in the examining area. Bill is given a hospital gown and I help him change into it and then get up onto the bed.

A few minutes later, Dr. Kong-Ting comes in holding a chart with the triage forms and the test result copies that we had brought. She is tall, certainly, by Asian standards, almost statuesque. With a professional efficiency mellowed by a soft voice, she asks Bill to describe why he is here. He looks to me a bit plaintively so I interject with the crib-note version of his last few months, focusing on the intense fatigue and abdominal pain. I mention the weight loss in passing.

She begins to feel around his stomach area and asks almost immediately, "How long have you been bloated like this?" The question surprises me. I have been so focused on the extent of weight loss that I had not recognised what she saw right away. Her examination lasts only a moment or two longer and then she says that she'll make arrangements for a variety of tests right away.

Bill lies back on the bed and closes his eyes. I take the opportunity to slip out of the room and approach her at the nurses' station where she is writing on his chart.

"Excuse me, but is the bloating that you asked about related to the ascites that's highlighted in the ultrasound report?"

I'm expecting an abrupt response because she is clearly working at a feverish pace. But she looks at me reassuringly patiently and says, "Yes."

"Do you have any idea what that might mean?"

"It could indicate the presence of a tumour."

I was standing on the small landing halfway up the flight of stairs between the dance floor and the balcony lounge. This was my preferred place to people-watch at the Manatee. You got a good view of the dancers to see who was dancing with whom. You could easily move downstairs to join them if the DJ threw on Donna Summers or Gloria Gaynor. Likewise, you had ready access to the upstairs bar if you got thirsty. I was a regular at the Manatee on Sunday evenings. It was the end of the weekend and people went there just to have fun with friends free from the Friday and Saturday night dating pressure. The place didn't have a liquor licence, but that didn't seem to be a deterrent. It was always packed, especially on Sunday evenings in those heady days of the mid-1970s. Many gay men in Toronto and from small towns within driving distance had their own exhilarating variation of the coming-out story where they opened the door of the Manatee, paid the cover fee, and then walked in and were blown away by their first-ever sight of a sea of male pulchritude bumping and grinding to the reigning disco divas.

"Would you like to dance?" asked a hesitant voice behind me.

I turned around on my little perch and found myself face-to-face with my current number one "untouchable," my category for guys who were so good-looking that they couldn't possibly ever notice a nerd like me.

"Okay," I mumbled. He headed down the steps and I followed, hoping that my friends would see whom I was accompanying out onto the dance floor.

There was always that dreaded moment as the song was coming to an end when you would fret about whether Mr. Perfect would signal that he was up for another dance or he would nod thanks and wander off. My Mr. Perfect seemed slightly hesitant. Turned out his tentativeness had nothing to do with his own intentions but with trying to discern whether I was going to nod and leave. I was totally oblivious to *his* reality: that he had been smitten with me since he first saw me and it had taken him six months to summon the courage to ask me for this first dance. Unbeknownst to me, he used to come up and stand as close as he dared behind me just to get a whiff of my scent and then would be so overcome with emotion (a.k.a. passion) that he would have to leave the club.

Fortunately, our mutual indecisiveness lasted long enough to get us over that hurdle and into the next song. After a few slightly less stressful transitions from piece to piece, he took the next big step. He held out his hand and said, "My name is Bill." Oh my God! When someone introduced himself to you at a gay club, it was a pretty good sign that he was interested in you.

I shook his hand in a state of panic. Do I use one of my clubbing pseudonyms so useful when you expect that you're going to want to give the guy the slip in a while? When I heard "David" come out of my mouth, I realised that I was prepared to bet all my chips.

"So, where do you and your friends like to go for fun?" he asked. To launch into an actual conversation was another big step in our primordial courting rituals. My heart was pounding as I tried to think of something to say that he might find interesting and thus postpone his inevitable discovery of my inherent nerdishness.

"Oh, New York, I guess," I said flippantly. I didn't know where that came from, but it sounded sort of sophisticated to me and I hoped might intrigue him enough to keep this moment from ending. While I thought I was sounding urbane, he was shattered. This idol that he had been mooning over for months was no more than your run-of-the-mill pretentious little prick. Thank goodness he didn't turn on his heels and walk away. We continued to talk and my nervousness must have subsided enough to allow a less insecure David to emerge.

Before parting, we agreed to meet the next Sunday night at the Manatee. I arrived just after it opened at 9:00 p.m. and hung around, increasingly despondent as I waited for him to show up. Finally, a couple hours later, he came sauntering through the door in jeans and plaid shirt, having just driven into town in his pick-up truck from a weekend building his cottage up north. You don't get a gay fantasy more potent than that. We danced and talked some more that evening, and then he asked me if he could take me out to a theatre play on Tuesday.

Forever thereafter, we considered that Tuesday evening, August 17, 1976, our first date and celebrated it every succeeding year as our anniversary. By Friday of that week, we were living together.

She's as good as her word. Within minutes a male nurse, coincidentally called William, appears at our room, draws back the curtain, and declares that we are off to the X-ray department.

The modern hospital bed is a marvellous invention. William pulls the plug out of the wall socket, taps the foot brakes to release them, and wheels Bill out into the corridor. No need to awkwardly transfer from bed into a wheelchair or other mobility device. I scurry to catch up to the 'William and William show' after remembering to retrieve Bill's valuables. People distracted by crises apparently make easy prey for pickpockets and skulking thieves—who'd have thought.

The X-ray technician is laughing on the phone as we enter. Bill takes that as his cue. Perfect setting for his joke-du-jour.

As soon as she hangs up, Bill declares, "I have a joke for you." No hello. No *is this going to hurt?* Just right to the point.

"Okay," she says, obviously a little startled at this unique greeting.

"A woman takes her dead duck into the vet. 'I think my duck is dead but I want to make sure,' she tells the doctor. 'Okay, put him up on the examining table.' The vet gives the duck a quick going-over and confirms the woman's suspicions.

"'Yup, you're right. Dead duck,' he chuckles.

"'That wasn't a very detailed analysis,' the woman complains. 'Don't you need to do more tests to make sure?' The vet sighs, opens the side door and motions. In saunters a large Labrador retriever. The vet points toward the duck and the dog hikes himself up on his hind legs and sniffs the duck from top to bottom. The dog looks at the vet, shakes his head, and exits back through the open door ... You're sure you haven't heard this one?" Bill asks the technician.

"No, really I haven't. Go on."

I'm feeling a little awkward. This is a busy hospital. There is likely a list of critically ill patients scheduled for X-rays today. And here my lover is spending precious minutes telling a joke while the high-priced technology sits idly waiting. But I learned long ago not to interrupt Bill when in full flight, correct him in public, or kick him under the table. Such gestures were always counterproductive with him, to my usual embarrassment.

He continues, "The duck woman is more than a little taken aback. 'What the #/*! was that? I want the best medical advice you can give me.'

"'Okay,' mutters the vet and opens the door again and in wanders a cat, jumps up on the examining table, and sniffs the duck for several minutes. The cat looks at the vet, shakes her head, and walks out of the room. 'Definitely dead,' concludes the vet.

9

"'I give up, just give me my bill,' the exasperated woman demands. The vet types into his computer and out shoots the bill. The woman shrieks in horror. 'Four hundred fifty dollars for telling me that my duck is dead. This is outrageous!'

"'Well, lady, if you had been satisfied with my initial exam the cost would have only been fifty. But you insisted on the full assessment. The lab report cost two hundred dollars and the CAT scan was another two hundred.'"

Pause. Then the technician's eyes light up as she puts together the punch line and that cackling laughter we had first heard when entering the X-ray room resumes.

I only kicked Bill under the table once.

When we first started living together thirty-three years ago, we both had sets of friends who were anxious to meet and pass judgment on the new boyfriend. We were later to recognize that a couple of his friends and a couple of mine had fancied themselves as potential partners for each of us, so they were none too excited about the newcomer.

One of these jealousies came close to precipitating an early tragedy. A week after we began our life together, Bill and a friend of his were at the rooftop pool of my apartment building. Bill had a house in another part of the city, but for convenience we had chosen to stay in my downtown apartment. This particular late summer day, I had to go out of town for a family event so Bill invited his friend over to enjoy the pool and sundeck. As they lay in the sun with Bill gushing over his new relationship, his "friend" told him he had some bad news. He told Bill that I was just stringing him along as a summer fling. I already had a partner. He was from Montreal and would be returning to Toronto in September at which point Bill would be tossed out of my apartment and my life. Bill was so devastated by the news that he actually considered jumping off the roof of the thirty-story building. As he retold the story in subsequent years, he would say that he was dissuaded from jumping by the image of the mess the fall would make out of his muscular, sculpted body. I knew that this macabre sense of humour masked an emotionally horrific experience he had had. Once I got home and convinced him of the falseness of his friend's accusation, we banned him from our lives, never to see him again (until he showed up at Bill's memorial service).

But back to under-the-table kicking. One evening, around the same time, we were having dinner at the apartment of a friend of mine who was expounding rather pretentiously on a subject about which Bill knew a great deal more than my friend. Eventually, Bill had had enough and told our dinner host that he didn't know what he was talking about. They started to argue. I, wanting my new boyfriend to make a good impression on my friends, nudged his foot under the table. I thought that that was a universally understood signal for shut up. But no, Bill continued on dismantling my friend's logic with ever more searing critiques. So I tapped his leg harder. Actually, I suppose it qualified as an under-table kick, at which point Bill turned to me and said, "Don't kick me under the table. I can say whatever I want. Just because we are boyfriends doesn't mean that you own me or can control me."

Right. Lesson learned.

After the X-ray is finished and the technician thanks Bill for the new joke, she pages an orderly to deliver us to the next testing site. Bill's bed is wheeled to a distant wing in the hospital and we are placed in the corridor queue for a CAT scan. There are several patients ahead of us, but the line moves pretty expeditiously and within fifteen minutes or so a technician comes into the hall and asks Bill if he is William Conklin. This time I am not allowed to go into the room with him but am directed to a nearby waiting room.

I wonder if he is telling her the dead duck joke.

For the first time today, Bill and I are separated. I have nothing to do but sit and wait. And think.

I replay the day's activities in my mind. It has been frenetic since Bill's early morning wake-up call. Because of the pace, I have not digested the implications of the activities. We are here at the hospital because Bill's doctor was concerned about the most recent tests results. We are now in the medical imaging department because the emergency room doctor was concerned about what we told her about Bill's recent history and about what she saw when she examined him.

Maybe we are finally going to get some solid answers as to what is going on with Bill.

But now as I sit here wondering what the CAT scan may show, I find myself having qualms about whether I really want to know after all.

We were always pretty candid with each other, certainly about the important things. If either Bill or I had a problem, whether it was physical, emotional, or spiritual, we let each other know what was going on.

There was one instance when I was determined to abrogate that transparency principle. On Maundy Thursday 1993, my doctor told me that I had tested positive for HIV. Sometime earlier, I had been careless about taking adequate precautions when looking after a friend of ours who was dying of AIDS. I was cleaning him at his apartment after a particularly messy session of bloody diarrhoea. I had a cut and I wasn't wearing protective gloves. He was emotionally distraught and I thought that if I put on gloves, it would make him feel even more ostracised than he was already.

I had forgotten about the incident.

The angst that I now experienced on receiving the news that I was HIV-positive was multidimensional. Of all the implications, my biggest worry was how Bill would react. I knew that he loved me intensely and that he would be traumatised by the prospect of me suffering what in those days was still anticipated to be almost certainly an excruciating deterioration to death. I couldn't stand the prospect of inflicting such pain on him. So I resolved not to tell him. We always practiced safe sex so I knew I posed no threat to him.

That evening we went to a Maundy Thursday worship service with a friend at a high Anglican parish. The music was exquisite. My internal turmoil was wrenching.

I was able to maintain my personal vow of silence for all of twenty-four hours. By Friday evening, I could no longer preserve this secrecy. It was too profound a deception. After dinner, I made coffee and as we sat down in the living room, I said that I had something to tell him. He looked at me with benign curiosity. I hesitated. Not that I was reconsidering my decision, but I wanted to relish for a moment longer this time in our lives when he would be in ignorant bliss.

"I'm HIV-positive."

Silence.

Then an anguished cry burst forth from the depths of his being. I hugged him as we both dissolved in tears.

I was back at work the Tuesday after the Easter holiday weekend. About midday, a delivery man walked into my office and handed me a long white box. I sat staring at it for several minutes and then slowly undid the ribbon and lifted the lid. A dozen red roses. The card read, *I will always love you. Bill.* To this day, that card and the dried rose petals sit on my desk.

It is taking forever to get the results of the tests. We have been back in the room in the emergency department since just after lunch hour. It is now nearly 5:00 p.m. I am grateful to see that Dr. Kong-Ting is still around. She is busy attending to other patients. I am hesitant to pester her so I go over to the nurses' station and ask one of them if they have any way of finding out how much longer we will have to wait. She says that she'll check with the doctor. The nurse comes into our room a little while later and says that she doesn't know what the hold-up is, but the doctor has spoken to the medical imaging department and they are working on the report. It shouldn't be too much longer.

Bill has been sleeping on-and-off in the bed. I have worked my way through this morning's paper, though if you asked me what I read, I'd be hard pressed to tell you. It's strange how you can read pages of a newspaper or book but your mind is somewhere else altogether. During this afternoon's waiting, my mind is not on anything specific. It is not on what I am reading. Nor is it on the circumstances that have led us to be here in this place. It is just wandering distractedly around in a murky ether, awake but not aware.

The doctor pokes her head in the room and says that it shouldn't be much longer. The report is on its way. Then just as quickly as she appeared, she disappears, off attending to another patient. I let Bill sleep. No sense in waking him until we have something.

From our room, I have a clear view of the nurses' station. A few minutes later, Dr. Kong-Ting is back at the nurses' station sitting at the counter, head buried in a file. *Please let it be Bill's.* She looks up and straight into our room. Our eyes meet for a second. She gets up and heads toward us. I think this is it. I am sitting by Bill's bed and now reach over and rub his arm to wake him up. Maybe he hasn't been asleep because he opens his eyes immediately and seems totally alert.

Dr. Kong-Ting strides into our room. I take ahold of Bill's hand. She pulls the curtain across the doorway to provide privacy for this conversation. I don't have time to reflect on whether this is significant. Standing at the foot of the bed and with a deliberation that is simultaneously efficient and compassionate, she looks directly at us and speaks in a slow measured pace.

"We have the results of the CAT scan finally. The report took hours to prepare because there was so much to document. It is twenty-six pages long. I'm very sorry to have to tell you that it is very, very bad news. Our diagnosis is pancreatic cancer, stage four. There are indications that the cancer has spread from the pancreas into the liver, the lungs, and the lymph nodes."

I am speechless. I turn my head slowly and look at Bill. He seems serenely placid, his face betraying no shock whatsoever. It's not that he has gone catatonic. Rather, he is looking directly into my eyes and calmly and lovingly asks, "Are you alright?"

"Noooooooooooooooooooooooooooooooooooooooo," I shout.

Christmas at the cottage was usually straight out of a Hallmark card. Lots of snow. Crackling fire in the hearth. Our stockings hung from the mantel. Presents under the decorated tree. A picture-perfect and romantic holiday.

That was until the Christmas of 1985.

We came up from the city on December 22. The car was loaded with all the provisions for the festive week, including wrapped gifts for each other, turkey and stuffing resources, a copious supply of eggnog, and the requisite Southern Comfort. Even Rufus our cat was snuggled in his carrying case in the car's back seat.

It was dark by the time we pulled up at the end of our lane where our snowmobile and sled were parked. There had been plenty of fresh snowfall over the preceding week. The county road was ploughed but our private lane never was during the winter, hence the need for the snowmobile. It was about a mile from the road into the cottage, a very long mile that year.

As Bill began unpacking the car, I went to start the snowmobile. Nothing. I fiddled with the choke and primed the engine again. I turned the ignition key again and again. We had put in a new battery recently and there was adequate gas in the tank. But some essential element of combustion magic was missing.

The nearest village garage was an hour away and would be closed by now anyways. And this was prior to the days of cell phones.

We figured that we had no choice but to start hauling the supplies into the cottage by hand. We prioritised what we thought most essential, Rufus included, and headed off into the moonless darkness. The fresh snow was so deep that we would sink down past our knees with every step.

We finally arrived at the cottage. Bill started a fire in the woodstove while I headed out for a second load, this time wearing the snowshoes that we kept in the shed. Snowshoes work well but they are an exhausting form of mobility especially when you are carrying more than just your own body weight. The round trip from cottage to car and back to cottage took me over an hour. By the time I got back to the now-toasty cottage, I was so exhausted my leg muscles were twitching uncontrollably. I wanted to get the remaining supplies before they froze but Bill insisted that I rest for a while first. I collapsed onto the bed and immediately fell sound asleep.

Bill knew that I would be fretting about what was left in the car as soon as I awoke. Even though he was at least as tired as I, he donned his snowmobile suit again and headed back out. By the time he had gotten another load and was trudging back toward the cottage, he was too tired to walk and had to crawl dragging the bags behind him. He would later describe how he would stop, lie on the snow and rest periodically, but not allow himself to put his head down because he knew that he could too easily fall asleep right there and then. And likely never wake up. He eventually made it back to the cottage in agonising pain while I snored in bed.

During the night, he would wake from time to time in panic and need reassurance that he was indeed safe in bed and not still on the trail hallucinating that he was safe in bed.

That was the night we almost died in the woods.

The next day, shaken and demoralised, we carried Rufus back to the car and drove home to the city. We left our gifts and other supplies to be retrieved when we returned in the spring. We sold the cottage.

Dr. Kong-Ting asks Bill whether he wants to be admitted right away though she cautions that since it is now late Friday afternoon none of the specialist departments will be functioning again until Monday.

Bill and I look at each other and reply almost in unison, "No, we're going to go home."

Over the past month or so, Bill and I had broached the hypothetical possibility that there might be something seriously wrong and we had agreed that in such an event we both would want him to be cared for at home. Thank God for my doctor, John Goodhew. During my past few monthly appointments, I had been venting to him my anxiety about Bill's deteriorating health and John had alerted me to the wide range of health services now available to care for people in their own home. I had relayed the information to Bill and so we both felt that there was a viable alternative to having him hospitalised, at least for the time being.

Dr. Kong-Ting excuses herself, saying that she will try and set up an appointment for us to come back in on Monday and see Dr. Bin in the oncology department. I help Bill get out of bed and while he changes from the hospital gown back into his street clothes, I slip over to the nurses' station and hover while Dr. Kong-Ting talks quietly on the desk phone. I see that she is reading from Bill's CAT scan report into the receiver. I assume that it's Dr. Bin on the other end.

She looks up, nods at me, and says, "Thank you very much," into the mouthpiece. She hangs up. "Yes, he will see Bill on Monday afternoon. Is 2:00 p.m. okay for the two of you?" I notice and am gratified anew how she has been treating us as a couple all day.

"Yes, that's fine. Can I ask you a quick question? Is it your assumption that this is basically inoperable?" *Did these words really come out of my mouth?*

"I'm afraid because it has spread so much, surgery is not going to be possible." She's being candid. I appreciate that, I guess. I feel like I'm on an out-of-control train and I'm transfixed, watching this unreal conversation flash past the window. "Dr. Bin will be in a better position to explore treatment options with you on Monday. What about painkillers in the meantime? I can prescribe pretty much whatever you think he would want. Something like Percocet?"

Bill has always hated medications. With multiple allergies, he's very sensitive and invariably experiences awful side effects. I gave him cough medicine one time that had DM (Dextromethorphan) in it and he had hallucinations for days afterwards. He revoked my nursing certificate then and there.

"He generally avoids medication so I think maybe something effective but fairly benign. How about Tylenol 3? But definitely not with codeine."

We drive home in silence, stopping to fill the prescription just as the pharmacy is closing. Back in the parking garage at our Toronto condo, we go through our usual routine of my hauling the wheelchair out of the trunk and then steadying him while he transfers himself from the car seat into it. There are a few other people on the elevator as we ride up to our floor. How can they be so nonchalant? Don't they know that this is apocalypse now? I want to scream but I stand there mute, massaging the handles of the wheelchair.

One way or another, we marked the major transitions in our lives. The happier ones, we invariably celebrated with parties. Over the years, Bill and I did a lot of entertaining. We enjoyed hosting people in our home. Call it the Adelle-Lillian gene. We both could recall many grand soirées organised by our mothers.

In December 2000, we gathered friends and family for a three-fold celebration: the inauguration of a new millennium, the year of my fiftieth birthday, and the cusp of the year of our twenty-fifth anniversary. We began the planning early and soon realised that the scope of our ambitions would strain the physical capacity of our country house in Stratford as well as the energies that we could bring to the food preparation. We already had a trip to Paris scheduled for late November and didn't fancy coming home from a week of Louvre-D'Orsay-Pompidou-Garnier-Bastille and having to throw ourselves into canapé recipes.

The solution—outsource the work to a hotel. A block from our Stratford house stood the venerable Queen's Inn. The edifice may have seen better days but the dining room had a cosy atmosphere with large cantilevered windows draped in red velvet, enough tables to seat one hundred plus, a parquet section of the floor big enough for the dancing styles of a range of ages, and a kitchen that could assemble a grand buffet that was equal parts tasty and tasteful. The multiple groups of friends that we were inviting from Toronto could stay overnight right there at the hotel, relieving us of any obligation to convert our house into a one-night bed-and-breakfast. With characteristic queenly fastidiousness, we worked out the minutiae of details with the hotel's catering manager and then left for Paris.

Stratford was blanketed with a fresh snowfall on the party night, not enough to cause a problem for the out-of-towners making the drive but sufficient to project a charming seasonal ambiance with all the Christmas lights strung along the main street. An hour or so before the party began, Bill and I walked the block from our house carrying our tuxedo suit bags and checked into the room that we had reserved for ourselves. Of course, we needed a room of our own to allow for the change of clothes from formal dinner wear to after-dinner-let-loose-and-party wear. As the hosts, we had to set a high standard.

It was a wonderful party. Everyone thought so. Late in the evening, Bill and I circulated around the room with a tray teeming with simple and elegant Christmas decorations that we had bought in Paris to give to our guests as a memento of the evening. I treasure a photograph from the party of my parents dancing arm in arm, Mom with the Christmas corsage on her wrist that we had bought for both our mothers. It was the last dancing occasion before Mom's deteriorating mobility put an end to that post-retirement form of exercise.

The one sour note (literally) of the evening was the DJ who we had hired supposedly on good recommendation. I thought his selection of dinner and dancing music was okay. My partner didn't. At times, Bill was almost apoplectic. But sufficient wine and the effusiveness of our guests, who were clearly enjoying themselves mitigated his distress, for the most part at least. When I or any friend referred to that party in subsequent years, Bill would say, "Remember that fucking DJ?"

Once we get into the apartment, Bill goes straight to bed. He's exhausted. I close the bedroom door and promptly collapse on the living room floor, weeping silently.

I've got to tell somebody but I can't. I wouldn't be able to get the words out. I go into the library and sit down at the computer, open my e-mail programme, and write the following message.

There's no easy way to break this news.

As you know, Bill has not been well for several months. We've just spent twelve hours at the hospital. Bill has been conclusively diagnosed with extensive and seemingly rapidly progressing cancer in the pancreas with indications of nodes in the liver, lungs, and possibly lymph glands. Initial indications from the emergency department doctors and other consultants inform us that it is likely inoperable. We

*don't know what the time frame is. We'll get more of an idea
from an oncology specialist who we see Monday afternoon.
We are home for the weekend.
I am hopeful that as much as possible he'll be able to
stay at home with the various supports that are available.*

Love, David

*P.S. E-mail messages are welcomed but I don't think
that we can handle visits or phone calls right at the moment.
I hope you understand.*

From my address book, I insert the names of our closest friends and family. I press "send." It's 7:09 p.m. The message, these words, this diagnosis, goes out to a small network of our loved ones. It can't be retracted. Now, it feels real. It is real.

Bill bought me my first computer. Many were the days that he rued that generosity with the refrain, "Are you on your bloody computer again?!"

It was around 1986 and I had begun my first book. I was working full-time on environmental education and advocacy for The United Church of Canada. Even though the focus of my writing related directly to this area of responsibility, producing a book was not part of the mandate of my portfolio. But I had been bit by the writing bug. I enjoyed putting ideas together and finding ways to articulate them in ways that were both conceptually challenging and popularly accessible.

The one tedious part was the physical process of pen on paper— writing a sentence, rethinking the phrase, scratching it out, and reorganising the thought with arrows and scribbles that inevitably left a Jackson Pollock on the page.

Bill could sense my growing passion to communicate through the written word. As on countless occasions over our life together, he took a pragmatic and personally sacrificial step to encourage me. A laptop computer was not inexpensive in those early days and his income was modest, cobbled together from his part-time music teaching, a few morning hours staffing a nearby antique store, and cleaning friends' apartments.

His gift of technological wizardry was a godsend for me. It allowed me to dispense with the reams of yellow foolscap that had been cluttering our dining room table every evening and weekend. Perhaps that was his real agenda. He deplored clutter on tables and countertops. In later years, he adopted Edwina's famous *AbFab* line, "Surfaces, sweetie darling, surfaces! I must see my surfaces!"

I eventually finished that first book, *Caring for Creation: The Environmental Crisis, a Canadian Christian Call to Action*. Short, snappy titles for books have never been my forte. This published work was the first of many more books, journal contributions, magazine articles, and private literary endeavours created on that first laptop and its successive generational replacements.

I was never able to forget that it was Bill whose generosity made that beginning possible. Of course, he didn't let me.

About an hour later, I'm at my computer reading with misting eyes the e-mail responses from family and friends that are starting to come in. "We're devastated." "It can't be true." "What can we do?"

I'm roused from my communion with the computer screen by totally out-of-context noises coming from the bedroom. Bill has woken up and he's laughing. Not a little giggle but hearty robust laughter. I run into the bedroom. His eyes are radiant.

"My God, I don't believe it. You won't believe it. I've just been having the most unbelievable dream." More laughter. He's shaking.

I leap onto the bed and grab his arm. "Tell me. Tell me. What's happening? Are you okay?"

"Okay? I'm incredible. I've never felt so incredible."

Gasping for breath, he tries to put words to his exhilaration. "I've just been walking in the garden with Jesus. It was so wonderful. We were joking and kibitzing. David, he told me that I looked so sexy. And my God, was he hot too."

I don't know whether to laugh or cry. I'm awestruck. How do I pivot from a day of shock to this? What is this? Is Bill for real?

Calming down a degree, he looks me straight in the eyes and says, "Don't worry, I haven't gone bonkers. This is really wonderful. Honestly, it's going to be okay. Jesus says that I have nothing to worry about or feel guilty about. Everything is forgiven. I should drop any of the burdens that I've been carrying. I'm loved. He loves me. He's ready for me. Everything is going to be okay. The pain will be over. I'm going soon."

He stops and takes a long, deep breath. I'm crying with joy.

Bill had been in spiritual agony. A few weeks earlier, he had said that he knew he was going to hell. He dropped the comment offhandedly, probably not sure how I would react or whether I would take him seriously. But his demeanour bespoke the depth of his despair. I pressed him. It didn't take much encouragement to get him to talk. He felt that he was teetering on a fragile precipice. Below was a chasm of anguish.

"What are you talking about?" I tried to sound light but not flippant.

"I'm going to hell. I'm sure of it."

"You can't really believe that. You're a good person. You've always been a good person. And you have such a profound faith. You believe in God and in Jesus. You're the one who keeps emphasising how important it is to nurture a relationship with the Holy Spirit."

"That's not it." He hesitated before continuing. "It's because I was responsible for my parents' death. I killed my parents, both of them."

He had alluded to this before. It was irrational. But he believed it.

When his father was dying of cancer in Stratford Hospital in November 1998, Bill had told the nursing staff that his father's favourite breakfast was rolled oats. It was his morning staple at home, prepared by Bill's mom. That was an easy request to accommodate in the hospital. So from then on every morning, Bill Sr. would get hot rolled oat cereal on his breakfast tray. Until his last morning. It wasn't the cancer that actually killed Bill Sr. It was the rolled oats. He choked on it while feeding himself one day before Bill and his mom arrived for their morning visit.

Bill felt that he had killed his father because he had suggested to the nurses that his father would like rolled oats.

In March 2007, we had to rush Bill's mother to the hospital after she had collapsed at home so weakened by her chronic congestive heart failure. The doctors put her on oxygen and she seemed to stabilise for a couple days. But one evening, she had some kind of respiratory seizure. They immediately moved her to the intensive care unit and inserted a respirator. I had never seen anyone on a respirator until then. The sight of a tube lodged down her throat pumping oxygen into her lungs looked uncomfortable in the extreme. She was in agony. They had to tie her hands to the bedsides to prevent her from trying to remove it. It was awful to see her in such distress. We tried to comfort her with platitudes about this being best for her. She would have none of it. Despite her limited capacity to talk because of the horrendous plastic tubing scraping against her vocal chords, she made it clear to us that she wanted it out. She didn't want to live like this. Bill pleaded with her that it was the only thing keeping her alive at this point. Her lungs were so filled with fluid that she couldn't survive without it. She knew that, but it wasn't worth it to her. She told Bill she was ready to go, to die. She wasn't afraid. She just wanted the wretched contraption out of her throat. After two long days and nights, Bill finally acquiesced and told the doctors to remove the respirator. Convinced that Adelle and Bill were fully aware of the consequences, they removed the respirator and we moved her to the palliative care wing. Five hours later, after we had all been able to say our good-byes, her breathing became very shallow. She closed her eyes and died.

Bill felt that he had killed his mother because he had given the green light to remove the respirator.

That was Bill's guilt for which he was convinced he was condemned. He had killed his parents. No amount of rational argument on my part or attempt at theological justification could dissuade him. He had no spiritual peace.

That all changed with his walk in the garden with Jesus on the evening of Friday August 7.

Chapter Two—Saturday, August 8

Bill's dream last night has not faded with this morning's dawn. As we begin the day after the diagnosis, he is as vibrant as when he awoke from his walk in the garden with Jesus. We pick up our conversation from where we left off. He knows that he is going to die soon. He is not afraid. He is prepared, ready to move on. "I have never felt so content," he declares to me, speaking softly, and with conviction.

For as long as we have been together, my most regular prayer has been that he not suffer. For thirty-two of our thirty-three years, my concern was his MS and the fatigue and discomfort that it inflicted. Over the past six months, that focus on the chronic was displaced by something more acute as a mysterious force started to shave pounds off his body, consume his abdomen with intensifying pain, and drain what little energy the MS had not already robbed. As of yesterday, we now have a name for that demon. But even more than praying that he not suffer physically, I had started to pray this year that he be liberated from his spiritual angst. He was so convinced that he would be held responsible for patricide and matricide.

My prayer has been answered. As of last evening, he now has spiritual peace. More than that, he is joyful. This is no delusional state. He is lucid, articulate, and bubbling with enthusiasm equally for life, and, I guess, for his impending death, and whatever form of life is to follow. Given where he was and where he is now, given the profoundness of the transformation, this is what I call a miracle.

Though I am relieved with the transformation, I am not in the same place. I still cannot internalise the reality of the diagnosis. But this is his moment, and I am determined to do nothing to dampen his euphoria.

"I am so thankful that you are feeling the way you are," I say to him. I really do mean that so I can speak the words with no deception of self or other.

"I am going to die soon. It's not going to be long I'm sure. I feel sorry about leaving you, but, my God, we've had a good life together. How many people have had the kind of love that we have had and for as long as we have had? We've been truly blessed."

"We've had a great run. Thirty-three years."

"We've had a really great run."

We both felt slightly depressed and couldn't figure out why.

It was our last night in Cairo, a sultry June evening in 1980. While resting in bed, we could hear the cacophony of street noise. An early dusk light was filtering through the curtains. We would get up shortly and head out for dinner and a stroll, invariably ending the evening in a café.

We had accomplished all the spectacular tourist adventures that we had planned—riding camels around the pyramids of Giza, standing in awe before the Great Sphinx, passing hours studying the antiquities in the Egyptian Museum, visiting King Tut's tomb in the Valley of the Kings, wandering around the overpowering columns of the Temple at Karnak.

Then there were the surprises—a mystical, romantic felucca ride on the Nile at sunset with two gregarious boatmen well supplied with beer and hashish, and the not-so-pleasant heat stroke that Bill suffered after we had rather stupidly spent hours at desert ruins in the noonday sun.

Beyond the expected and the unexpected, what we enjoyed most were the evening strolls around the streets of Cairo ablaze with lights, music, smells, and noise. The cafés were always only populated by men, the women consigned to their homes by the still-rigid social separation of the genders. Invariably, if we glanced in and our eyes met any of the tables of friends, they would beckon us in, serve us coffee, and offer us a hookah. We spoke virtually no Arabic, though Bill with his lifelong fascination with languages had made sure that he picked up some basic greetings. Our spontaneous hosts spoke no English. Somehow we had wonderful conversations. The ambiance was one of generosity and camaraderie.

This, we realised, was why we were feeling sad that last evening in Cairo. An end was coming to our time in this exotic homoerotic ethos. Sort of like when a parting starts to loom, signalling the end of a decades-long romance.

Before I start eating supper, I pause to say grace. I'm alone at the dining room table as I have been for weeks now. For most of July, Bill had neither the strength nor the appetite to eat much. Occasionally, he could manage a few spoonfuls of oat bran cereal in the morning, perhaps half a bowl of chicken noodle soup for lunch or supper.

He is asleep in the bedroom tonight as I sit down alone at the table with a grilled chicken breast and steamed broccoli on the plate in front of me. But as I prepare to say grace, my isolation at the table is not depressing. There is not a fibre of despondency in me. Bill is in bed in the next room in a state of peace I could never have imagined possible. All day our conversation has been filled with laughter and joyfulness, reminiscing about places we visited, friends who have been part of our lives, and the many celebratory occasions when we hosted dinners for our parents at the various homes we have had in Toronto and Stratford.

And so even though it would seem like I should have an agenda for God and a challenging list of demands, I find myself just smiling and saying, "Thank you, thank you, thank you. For giving Bill the peace that now overwhelms him and that has exorcised the dual devils of guilt and fear. For the thirty-three years of sharing life with this wonderful man. For the fun we've had. For the enrichment of our countless experiences. For our homes, our families, our faith. Amen."

After eating, I clean up and peek into the bedroom to see if his bedside water glass needs refilling. He is looking out the window, eyes wide open.

"You're awake. Can I get you anything?"

"Maybe you can refresh my water. I think it's probably time to take another of those painkillers though I'm feeling pretty much okay at the moment. How are you doing?"

"Well, to tell you the truth, I can't stop smiling. I keep replaying our conversations today. When I went to say grace before supper, all that I could think of were reasons to be thankful."

"We are so much on the same page. I love you."

"I love you too."

We had seen *Don Giovanni* many times before. Our favourite production to date had been at the Royal Opera Covent Garden in London. But to see the Mozart classic, or just about any opera for that matter, at La Scala in Milan would be a dream come true. We had enjoyed performances in most major opera houses around the globe but had never been to the Mecca of the opera world.

While planning a trip to Italy, I checked out the performance schedule for La Scala and found that *Don Giovanni* was being performed just at the time that we anticipated being in Milan. Tickets became available online about six weeks before the date. So at 4:00 a.m. on the first day of sales, I was at my computer in our

Stratford home ready to log into the La Scala website at the moment that the box office opened at 10:00 a.m. Milan time. Busy. I hit the refresh button. "Website not available. Please try again later," in Italian, of course. Refresh. Refresh. Refresh.

For hours I tried to get through. Eventually, to my great relief I was successful. I navigated via the various links until I got to the date and performance that we were interested in. I selected the appropriate boxes for number of tickets and seating section and clicked "purchase." The hourglass icon rotated and rotated and rotated. Eventually, the order page cleared and I held my breath. "Sold out."

I had to break the bad news to Bill that we would have to be content on our stay in Milan with seeing da Vinci's *The Last Supper*, ogling the designer shops on Via Montenapoleone, and taking a cappuccino in La Galleria.

When we got to Milan, we tried to compensate ourselves by taking a tour of the famous opera house. That was interesting but decidedly second-best. Just before heading away from the building, we decided to check at the box office to see if there might possibly be any tickets returned for that night's performance. Bill approached the wicket and, drawing on the fruits of his Italian language studies, he asked about tickets. The clerk just laughed. Dejected, but not surprised, we turned away.

Outside the box office door, we caught sight of a very hot looking leather-clad young man perched on an expensive motorcycle. Or rather, he caught our eyes. He raised his shades and smiled at us. *The Italians are forward*, we thought. God bless them. We sauntered over, just to be hospitable of course.

"You looking for tickets?" he asked in English with a very sexy Italian accent.

It took us a moment to shift gears and then, after the initial disappointment, our mood brightened considerably. "You mean you have some for sale?" I stuttered.

"Well, of course." Duh. Bill and I looked at each other. Had we never heard of the world of scalpers?

We enjoyed the performance. We didn't find it as creative as the London production and Bill had some critique of Leporello's timing. But, my God, we were at La Scala. The acoustics were phenomenal and we got to gawk down on everyone below us. Mind you, we were sitting in the very, very, very top balcony and the seats had cost us three hundred US dollars apiece.

Money comes and money goes. Experiences like that stay with you. We would reference our La Scala night from time to time over the years. And be thankful.

Chapter Three—Sunday, August 9

The painkillers aren't working very well. He doesn't complain, but his brow is consistently furrowed, and his eyes squint.

"Were you able to sleep much?"

"Not really."

"Can I interest you in some hot cereal?"

"Ugh. No. But you know what I could go for?"

"What?"

"I'd love some juice, something really flavourful."

I'm flummoxed. He hasn't wanted anything other than water to drink for weeks. He thought anything else would irritate the spasming oesophagus that had been diagnosed. Oh, the good old days when that had been the only identified problem.

"I think the only thing that we have in is apple juice."

"No, I want something to really knock my socks off. Grapefruit or orange or tangerine."

I really want to be able to get him what he wants, but I don't want to leave him alone. He is losing muscle strength quickly and needs my help any time he has to get out of bed and to the bathroom.

Denny. He was the first friend to respond to Friday evening's town crier message reporting on Bill's diagnosis. Denny's e-mail had included the offer, "*If there is anything we can do, please don't hesitate to ask. Grocery shopping, drug store runs, cleaning, any type of task—we're there within minutes of your call.*"

I'm on the phone. "Hi, Denny, it's David. Sorry to be calling you on a Sunday morning."

"Oh, I'm so glad to hear from you. How are you guys? We've been thinking about you nonstop."

"Well, yesterday was actually a wonderful day. Bill's very much at peace with the idea of dying. It's been quite amazing. I'll give you full details, but right now I need to ask a favour."

"Anything."

"You offered to run an errand if we needed, and we need one. Bill's gotten a sudden craving for some really flavourful fruit juice. And he says none of that no-name schlock. Something really good."

"I can just hear him," Denny laughs. "I'm on my way as we speak. David's off at church with the car so I'll be biking. I should be able to be there with the supplies in fifteen or twenty minutes."

"Thanks. You're a darling."

Denny is at the door in record time. I let him in and we hug. Amazing how his extra bit of pressure and the slightly longer than usual embrace communicates a world of empathy and condolences.

I wipe my eyes and say robustly as we enter the bedroom, "The demanding patient is in here."

Denny puts the bags of juice down, gives Bill a big hug and starts chatting him up with his characteristic vivaciousness. Not a scintilla of pity. As our first visitor since Friday's diagnosis, I'm relieved that he's striking with a note of everything-is-as-normal-as-ever. But as I stand quietly on the other side of the bed watching him joke with Bill, I think I can detect the ever-so-slight extra effort that he's exerting to keep himself calm and jocular. God love him.

A few weeks earlier, I was standing in front of the store shelves staring at the varieties of Jell-O. I was sure that he had said he wanted lemon jelly powder. I can't see any. There was orange and lime and several other flavours, but no lemon. Lots of lemon pie filling mix and lemon pudding, but he wanted the jelly powder. It's easier to digest, I guess.

Damn. I was desperate to get him what he wanted. I started to cry.

It was the stress of everything I suppose.

My Jell-O meltdown.

"I should make some phone calls," Bill says about midafternoon.

"What do you mean?"

"I mean I should make some phone calls. You know it's that new invention where you press some buttons and instantly you can talk to a real person miles away."

"Smarty. Do you need our phone directory?"

"No, I don't think so. Everyone who I want to talk to is on the speed dial."

I admire his courage. I realise that he wants to personally break the news to some people who he loves and who love him. There are a few friends who do not have e-mail and so have not been informed through the message that I sent out Friday evening. Then there are a couple of his family members with whom he is close. I'm relieved that he wants to call them because I felt it would be presumptuous for me to contact them.

He asks me to be on an extension. The first call is to his Aunt Marion, a sister of his father. Mame and Bill have a wonderful relationship and often chat on the phone. Next is his cousin Leslie, with whom he regularly reminisces about their childhoods together. He moves on to Joan, a longtime friend from the beach, and then three sets of friends we met in Puerto Vallarta: Chrissie and David from Toronto, Eric and Stephen in New York, and Eric and Randy in Albany.

My role on the calls is to provide the explanatory details of the diagnosis. Bill finds that part too tedious. Besides, it's getting more difficult for him to speak loudly enough into the receiver to be heard. After the initial greetings, he gets to the point, and tells them why he's calling. He cues me and I provide the specifics. Then I back off and he takes over trying to help them through the shock. He is calm and reassuring. "I really am at peace with this. I'm going to be going to a place where there is no more pain. I don't want you to be sad for me. I love you very much."

It is not the kind of call one expects to receive on a Sunday afternoon. It is not the kind of call one ever wants to receive.

It was the only time I remember Bill Sr. saying grace.

Bill and I hosted innumerable family holiday dinners around our dining room table at the Stratford house. Most often it was with his and my parents. Sometimes we expanded the table to accommodate my brothers and their wives, nieces and their husbands.

But this Christmas dinner in 1997 was upstairs in Bill's parents' apartment with just the four of us. Bill Sr. had started treatment for cancer. He was quite weak and it was easier for Bill and me to come upstairs than for Bill Sr. and Adelle to come downstairs.

When Bill and I were looking for a house to buy in Stratford in 1991, we only considered duplexes because we conjectured that one or the other of our sets of parents might need accommodation and care as they aged. In 1992, we invited Bill Sr. and Adelle to live with us. I didn't realise at the time what a generous gesture that was on my Bill's part. There was history.

"I pray that the four of us will be sitting around this table again next Christmas," Bill Sr. said before we began our meal. A few words that bespoke a chasm bridged between my partner and his parents.

At Christmas 1998, we were three.

Some of the neighbours with whom we've become good friends come to visit in the evening.

Bill seems to be taking his diagnosis a lot easier than the rest of us. Teresa and John and Niki and Chris have limited success disguising their distress. Bill is the one trying to cheer us up. Since his dream, he's become quite evangelical. He spends much of their visit regaling them on how everything will be all right. God loves them.

They don't stay too long because it is evident that Bill is tiring. When they say good-bye to him, it feels like good-bye. Bill is asleep within thirteen seconds after they leave. I head back to the computer and send an update to the many family members and friends who have responded to my Friday night message.

Dear family and friends,

Thank you for all your messages of support, your prayers, and your love, which Bill and I feel surrounding us at this time.

Bill has weakened significantly over the weekend. Though physically very fragile, he is still quite lucid when he is awake.

The main message that I want to communicate is how profoundly at peace he is. Spiritually, emotionally, and psychologically, he is ready to go. He feels that will be soon.

We are both very grateful for our faith, for our life together, and for all of you who have been so much a part of our life.

I will be in touch again.

Love, David

Chapter Four—Monday, August 10

I am awake early after a fitful sleep. I look over at Bill. He appears peaceful. He is asleep, his breathing quiet and measured.

As the new reality of our lives asserts itself in my now fully awake state, I start making a mental list of tasks. We are supposed to see Dr. Bin, the oncology specialist at the hospital this afternoon, but I doubt that Bill will have the stamina for the trip. I don't know if his pronounced physical weakening of the past two days would have happened anyway or if he is yielding to the inevitable. I should call the hospital this morning and see if we can have a consultation with Dr. Bin over the phone.

I've got to get through to Bill's doctor. Because Bill is still officially his patient, Dr. Hii is the one who has to make a referral to the Community Care Access Centre in order to initiate in-home care. Bill clearly needs stronger painkillers than the Tylenol that I foolishly thought on Friday would be sufficient. While Bill is his patient, Dr. Hii is the only one who can prescribe something else.

I should go to the bank. There are many errands that friends can do, but there are some that they can't. A few weeks ago, Bill and I took the precaution of ensuring that our names were on each other's bank accounts. But I don't want to be battling any overlooked banking regulations at a time like this if I need to access some of the resources in his accounts. I figure it would be better if I transferred most of our collective funds into my account.

Then there is the funeral home. Last evening, I phoned Rosar-Morrison, which is just around the corner, and started the process verbally. But I'll need to make arrangements to meet with one of their staff in person and prepare a contract. Michael was helpful on the phone in explaining what I would need to do if Bill died precipitously. I would have to call 911 and the police, fire department, and EMS would have to come. I pray that it doesn't come to that—sirens, interrogations, invasive attempts at resuscitation.

I phone the hospital and talk to Dr. Bin's secretary. She couldn't have been nicer. He's on rounds this morning, but she assures me that he'd be absolutely willing to talk to us by phone rather than having us come into his office given Bill's weakened condition.

I call Dr. Hii's office but can only get the voicemail of Vi, his secretary. I leave a message explaining what happened at the hospital on Friday. They won't have heard yet because their office was closed on the weekend. I know that Vi is going to be upset. She and Bill have been good buddies.

I decide to call Ray, one of our retired friends who volunteered in a weekend e-mail to help out any way he could. Perhaps, he'd be willing to come to the apartment and stay here with Bill while I run some errands. I telephone. He's happy for something practical to do to help.

Bill is still asleep when Ray arrives. I explain that there's nothing much to do except to freshen Bill's water if he wants. I don't mention it to Ray, but I hope that Bill doesn't wake up and need help to get to the bathroom. Bill would find it humiliating to have to rely on someone other than me for such an intimate task.

I pretty much jog the three blocks to the bank. The last time Bill and I were in the bank, Bill was in the wheelchair, which startled the staff. They had seen him deteriorating over the past month but had not anticipated the sight of him in the wheelchair. I'm glad that John is available and I go to his wicket. Deanna sees me and comes over immediately to ask how he's doing. I tear up.

"We were at the hospital all Friday for more tests. It's cancer. Pancreatic. It's all through his body. He's at home, but the doctors don't think he probably has long."

Both John and Deanna are dumbstruck. In hushed voices they ask what they can do to help. I explain what I need to do this morning and they start to expedite the transfers immediately.

I open my bag and bring out a copy of Bill's will and give it to Deanna. I say to her, "It looks like the power of attorney may not be of use too much longer. You'd better have a copy of this. It names me as his executor and trustee. I thought I should give it to you now because I don't know when I'll be back in again. I'll be staying at home with him full-time for the foreseeable future."

I can't talk any longer. I'm using all my resources to maintain composure and I want to get back to the apartment. I thank them for their help and leave.

I stop into the funeral home and the secretary makes an appointment for one of their staff to come to our condo on Wednesday afternoon to do the prearrangement planning.

I've been down this road far too frequently in the past few years. Planning funerals for Mom, Bill's mom, Dad, and then Rick, my brother. Now Bill. It doesn't get any easier with repetition.

I was still working when Mom took a turn for the worse. She and Dad had been living in the nursing home in Waterloo for about three years. I used to provide her and the staff with a calendar of my travel schedule, highlighting the days that I would be coming to visit. I tried for once every two weeks at least. In between, Mom had become proficient at using the speed dial on her phone to call my cell phone, which I had programmed on the receiver as number 1.

Numbers 2 and 3 as well, in case her finger slipped. At the height of her need for the reassurance of contact, my cell phone bill registered about three hundred calls from her monthly.

According to the nursing home staff, the weekend before she died she kept asking them multiple times every day, "When does David get back?" I was due to return from a week of meetings in Europe on the Monday.

Monday evening, just after arriving home, they called. "Your mom has taken a turn for the worse. Any chance that you could come up?" I'm convinced that Mom had waited until she knew that I was back on the continent, and then let her body start to free the spirit. With Bill's blessing, I hopped in the car, and spent the next forty-eight hours at her bedside until she breathed her last on Wednesday evening at 11:30 p.m. I initiated the funeral planning. On the funeral weekend, my brothers and their wives arrived from Phoenix and New York. My nieces and their husbands hosted us in Kitchener. Bill took the bus up from Toronto. It was a big funeral. Mom and Dad had lots of friends in our hometown community of Kitchener-Waterloo. October 5, 2005. Thanksgiving Monday.

Bill's parents, Bill Sr. and Adelle, lived with us in our Stratford house from 1992 on. After Bill Sr. died of cancer in 1998, we had a nice memorial service for him with family gathered in a circle at the funeral home telling stories. Adelle lived on with us for another decade. She gradually started suffering from congenital heart failure and became fatigued and very short of breath. Since I had retired as of January 2007, I was able to stay in Stratford to look after her while Bill continued with his music students in Toronto. One night in early March, Adelle lost her balance and fell in the bathroom. I heard her call out my name and then a bang. I opened the bathroom door and she was on the floor unconscious, having hit her head on the sink on the way down. I couldn't move her and I was afraid to in case she had a broken bone or something. Calmly, amid my panic, I decided that the situation definitely warranted 911 and EMS. We got her to the hospital and she revived, but was soon transferred to intensive care where they inserted a respirator down her throat. After much pleading from her, Bill finally consented to have the doctors remove the respirator and she died peacefully within a few hours. Her Rebecca Lodge sisters organised a lovely memorial service for her a week later, and then Bill and I hosted in our home a celebration of her life on the May weekend closest to what would have been her eighty-seventh birthday. The house was filled with family members, friends of hers and of ours, and caregivers who had helped look after her. It was a good party—she would have enjoyed herself.

Two weeks after Adelle's death, I got a call from the nursing home in Waterloo eerily similar to the one about my mom a couple years earlier. "Your dad has stopped eating and drinking. We don't think that he can last much longer. You might want to come as soon as possible." The nursing home staff was wonderfully accommodating and set up a cot in Dad's room so that I could be with him twenty-four hours a day. Dad's heart confounded all of us by refusing to stop. He held on and on and on for two weeks more until April 20, 2007. Halfway through that vigil, my brother Rick and his wife Diane flew up from New York for the weekend. At one point, we had the phone up to Dad's ear with our brother Jim from Phoenix on the line. Though Dad wasn't able to talk, he was alert, and we, his three sons, had a last conversation with him together. Another big funeral with many of the same participants.

Rick's death was totally unexpected. He was thirteen months younger than me, and we had grown up pretty much as twins. In June 2008, he retired from a very responsible senior academic position in New York City. He was the author of a high school biology textbook used extensively throughout the state. In January 2009, he became overwhelmed by intense depression and took his own life. We were all traumatised. I organised one memorial service for him in New York City a week after his death and then a second in our family's hometown of Waterloo a couple months later.

Now in August 2009, I was starting the process of organising Bill's.

I am about to call Dr. Bin the oncologist. I decide not to wake Bill. It seems that he sleeps better during the day than at night, so I might as well leave him. He has accepted the diagnosis. He knows he's going to die soon. He doesn't seem to want details.

I'm not sure why, but I need to know everything. Dr. Bin's voice is calm. Seriously calm. He has the report from Friday's CAT scan and has obviously studied it.

"It is multiloculated."

"Pardon me?"

"Oh, sorry. That means that it has appeared in numerous locations. There is one large mass in the pancreas. There are lesions on both sides of the liver. Lung deposits. In the abdomen, the lymph nodes are enlarged."

"Bill has weakened dramatically over the past few days. Can you conjecture how long he has?"

"That's hard to tell, but it appears to be progressing rapidly. Perhaps a few weeks, not likely more than a few months."

Next up, I need to call Dr. Hii. I get Vi on the second ring. She says how terribly sorry she was to have gotten my voicemail message this morning. I know she really means it. She likes Bill a lot. She puts me right through to Dr. Hii.

By now, early afternoon, he has gotten a copy of the report from the hospital. He agrees to call in a prescription to our pharmacy for a stronger painkiller, Percocet. I explain that Bill and I both want to keep him at home. Dr. Hii asks me to call the Community Care Access Centre and have them fax him the referral form so that we can get assessed for home care.

Things are moving along.

I check in on Bill and he is awake. I report the progress so far.

"Can I have some more juice please?"

Of Denny's varieties, orange-tangerine is Bill's favourite. I bring it in and we jointly manipulate the straw to the right angle. Drinking directly from a glass is a thing of the past.

Two minutes later, the juice has reemerged and is all over the sheets, his T-shirt, and the floor. I guess that was too much, too fast.

"Maybe this would be a good time for a shower and then I can change the bed."

He has difficulty swinging his legs out of bed. With a little struggling, we get him sitting on the edge of the bed and use our practiced routine to lift him to his feet, my hands cupping his elbows and his hands grasping my arms. We maintain that grip while heading to the bathroom, me walking backward and him shuffling along. This is new. He didn't need this much help yesterday.

He manages to step into the shower. I'm nervous about leaving him alone in there, but he says he'll be alright. He can hold onto the grab bars. He mainly just wants to stand with the warm water splashing down over him. I race to strip and change the bed so that it's clean and dry before he's ready to get out of the shower.

We head back to bed and he falls asleep pretty quickly. Taking a shower can knock the stuffing out of you apparently.

In the early evening, we have two other sets of visitors—Peter and Eric from upstairs and Peter and Bob from down the street. There is something of a pattern now: soberness and a few tears at the door as I let them in, and then jocular conversation with Bill in the bedroom. It is getting more difficult to hear his side of it. His voice is softer and softer. Not by choice.

You gotta love irony.

Bill was always big on soft voices. He had the acute hearing of a musician and would feel physical pain if exposed to too much volume. He sometimes took ear plugs to movie theatres. One of his teacher lines if any children visiting in our home were getting too loud: "Inside voices, please! Inside voices!"

It had been over fifteen years since he had gone with me to any of the big gay dances. The volume of the music drove him nuts. The intensity of the bass bothered his heart. The dry ice elicited an allergic reaction. If he regretted missing out on the nightlife, he didn't say so. He had alternate ways of spending his evenings at home that he enjoyed much more.

Bill watched movies over and over again—at volume levels he could control. He had definite favourites. He would claim that he was a true connoisseur. Repetition didn't make for boredom.

- *The Talented Mr. Ripley*—Bill had a hard time watching Philip Seymour Hoffman in any later movies, he loathed his Freddie Miles character so much. He always turned the movie off when Tom Ripley (played by Matt Damon) and his seemingly meant-to-be boyfriend Peter Smith-Kingsley (played by Jack Davenport) were romantically sailing across the Atlantic. That's before Tom kills Peter. Big butch Bill preferred a happy ending.
- *The Women*—The original version from 1939, of course. "Norma Shearer is so sweet as Mary Haines. Why can't you be more like her?"

- *Gone with the Wind*—Bill loved Olivia de Havilland so much, especially in the carriage scene with Belle Watling, that he was called "Melanie" by many of our friends.
- *La Dolce Vita*—Don't ask me why. I don't get it. But Bill thought it was the best movie ever.
- *Back Street*—Actually this tied with *LDV* for best movie. "Watch how Susan Hayward tosses her head back. It's coming. It's coming. There it is! God, I wish I could do that."
- *Fight Club*—"Hot, hot, hot."
- *Bed of Roses*—He was never one for chick flicks, but this was an exception. He would actually get teary-eyed watching it. Only movie that I ever saw make him cry.

Chapter Five—Tuesday, August 11

Bang. "Owwwww. Ohhhhh. Ohhhhh."

I tear into the bedroom and Bill is lying in the foetal position on the floor at the foot of the bed. Then I see blood. He must have hit his head on the bedpost or cupboard on the way down.

Oh my God. "Don't move, darling. Just stay still for a moment. Catch your breath."

"Owwwww."

"Just relax. I'm going to lift your head slowly and slip this pillow underneath." His racing, laboured breathing starts to slow a bit. "Do you think you broke anything?"

"I don't know," he says through another moan.

I warm a washcloth and dab gently at the red on his forehead. I think it's only a surface scratch but broad enough to create a steady rivulet for a few minutes. "Does it hurt if I touch you here on your arm or anywhere along here on your legs?" He doesn't answer, which I interpret as a good sign.

I begin to climb down from my panic and say with more of a chiding voice than I should have, "What did you think you were doing?" Again no response. His eyes are closed. A sudden flashback to his mom's fall. "Bill. Bill. Can you hear me?"

"I can hear you just fine." He puts me in my place.

"Were you going to the bathroom?"

"Duh."

"Oh sorry. You should have called me. That's what the bell is for." The Marrakesh bell from the Jemaa el Fna market. I had bought it in 2001 when the UN Climate Summit was held in Morocco to convene the participants at an interfaith symposium that I chaired in my role with the World Council of Churches. I felt it would be a little more dignified than yelling. It had sat on my desk as a souvenir for years but over the past few weeks had found a new vocation as Bill's summoning tool.

"I thought that I could make it on my own."

"Okay, well it doesn't matter. The bleeding on your forehead seems to have stopped. Do you think we can get you up slowly?" I help him roll over onto his knees. Now it's not his wounded head but the increasingly sensitive abdomen that is causing him to moan. Eventually, mission is accomplished and he's safely back in bed. With trepidation and using as innocuous terminology as possible, I ask, "What if we started to use incontinence briefs?"

Pause. "Good idea."

That's it? No argument?

One of those pivotal turning points.

I've had my fair share of falls.

I fell in love with Bill on the dance floor at the Manatee.

I fell from grace one time when I chastised him in public for some minor etiquette indiscretion. He was furious that I had called attention to it in front of friends. My mea culpas went on for weeks. He eventually forgave but never forgot.

I fell asleep one time while we had dinner guests. Not a popular move with my cohost or the assembled party.

I slipped off a windsurfing board one time when we were vacationing in Cuba. I later noticed blood on the board and realised that I had scraped my shin. *No big deal*, I thought, until I remembered that sharks had been sighted in recent days in those waters.

I was forever falling for his practical jokes. One winter weekend at the cottage, I was trying to attract chickadees to the scratch grain that I held in my hand. They wouldn't come to me, but Bill had no such trouble. Within seconds of extending his arm, he had one and sometimes a couple perched on his winter glove, eating out of his palm. "I guess they can tell who is pure of heart," he teased me. He loved to retell the story to friends. Years later, he confessed to me that his handful of scratch grain had been spiked with his secret stock of sunflower seeds.

"You may be homosexual, but you can't be gay," he admonished me on countless occasions when I proposed a decorating idea that evidently abrogated the parameters of good design. Seeing the evidence in our contrasting contributions to the décor of our homes, I acquiesced to his better taste and fell in line.

"David, I don't want you coming in here all the time and disturbing me. I want to go and I'm ready to go. I can feel that I am fading, but every time you wake me, you disrupt the process. Sorry if it sounds harsh, but you've got to leave me alone so that I can slip away."

Do I love him enough to give him what he wants?

"But what if you really need something?" I stutter. "Like water. Speaking of which, you are due for another painkiller." I get a fresh glass of water and give him one of the newly arrived Percocets. I'm stalling for time.

"I can ring the bell if I need you."

"So, maybe this is it?"

"You know that I love you. We've had a wonderful life together. Thank you for everything that you have done to make it so great."

"I love you too and I want you free of this pain. So I guess this is good-bye, my darling."

"Good-bye, my love."

We hug. We kiss. I leave the room and close the door.

I go into the living room and pour myself a stiff midday Scotch.

For the next eight hours, I resist going back into the bedroom. Occasionally, I can't help myself and pry the door open slightly to see if there is some movement of the sheets that signals a heart still beating and lungs still breathing. I have plenty to keep myself occupied. There is no limit on how often I can circumnavigate the kitchen island with my nervous pacing. I have to keep Simon distracted with cuddles so that he doesn't stand meowing at the bedroom door. I surf the net for every website with information on indicators of end of life. I organise photos on my computer for use at an eventual memorial service. I doze from time to time on the sofa. I keep calling the CCAC to see if they have gotten the referral from Dr. Hii and when they can schedule an assessment person to visit us. Just in case we still need them.

Waiting sucks. We had just moved into our first condo. I put an LP of Mahler's *Resurrection Symphony* on the turntable and cranked up the volume to distract myself. I stared at the phone willing it to ring. Bill hadn't wanted me at the hospital when he broke the news to his parents. Or rather the "newses." Plural.

His father needed to go to New England for business, and he and Adelle were anxious to get on the road, but Bill convinced them to come see him first. He told them that it was important.

He opened with the MS. The doctors were pretty sure of the diagnosis. He then told them that he wasn't teaching full-time anymore. "There's more. I'm in love and I'm living with him. A man. I'm gay."

The phone rang. "You can come now," he said.

"Are your parents still there? Will I meet them?"

"No, they've left. They didn't take it well."

This evening I receive an e-mail message for Bill from my brother Jim in Phoenix:

Bill, why do we (me in particular) not express ourselves more deeply more often?

You have been a cherished family member since we first met you in David's Toronto apartment/condo so many years ago. At first, we were a surprised party to be sure! Mom and Dad, my wife and myself—I am not sure if the little girls were there or not, as the year escapes me (like so much else these days).

Anyhow, you have brought so much to our family. Your love, your caring, your sharing, and your sense of humor are an inspiration. David has been so very lucky to be exposed to you full-time, while we only have snippets to cherish. We regret having been so far away for so long and only experienced you way too infrequently and in moments far too short. Your focus on the little and not-so-little grandchildren is a testament to your loving nature.

When we spoke several Saturdays ago, after you had just started the twenty-day regimen with the meds for your oesophagus, you cracked a joke. I had mentioned that Mario, our oldest, is back in Afghanistan, and you commented on how drab the military uniforms are. You said, "If David and I had to wear those, can't you just see us adding some piping to spruce them up?" A slice of Bill I will always carry with me.

You have always been special, Bill, because you were you, and because you brought thoughtful, insightful conversation into the moment. Jaye and I feel a very profound loss in that we cannot express our deep love for

you in person at this time, but there will come a day when
we can again.

Around midnight, I slip into the bedroom and crawl into bed as stealthily as possible. Bill's been sleeping so soundly for hours, I'm trusting that I won't wake him. I lie motionless, intending to stay for just a few minutes.

Chapter Six—Wednesday, August 12

As I open my eyes, I can see through the bedroom shades that it's light outside. Oh jeez, how long did I sleep? Bill is in the same position he was when I came to bed last night. I watch the sheets for the telltale rise and fall motion. I can't detect any. His left arm is lying on top of the covers. I touch it gingerly. It's stone cold. I pull my hand away and just lie there absorbing the implication.

I get out of bed and walk around to his side. My eyes fill with tears. I kneel down beside the bed, wrap my arms around him, and start to bawl.

"*What the fuck are you doing?*" he screams. He's wide awake and he's livid.

I jump back, almost knocking the bedside table over. I stammer, "I thought you were gone. I thought you were dead. I'm sorry, I'm sorry, I'm sorry."

He's still yelling. "I was almost gone! I was on my way! And now I'm back! Damn you!"

My grief of a moment ago morphs into despair, and the tenderness of yesterday's good-byes seems like a distant dream.

Bill and I had remarkably comparable dreams of my mother a few months after she died in 2005. She was dressed identically in both dreams, an elegant black dress with a string of pearls around her neck.

In Bill's dream, Mom was sitting cross-legged. Her mobility difficulties and concomitant weight gain after retirement were so severe that she hadn't been able to sit like that for years. In the dream, Bill reached out, grabbed the toe of one of her patent leather shoes, gave it a little tweak, and said something to the effect of, "You rascal, you look ready for a night of dancing on the town." She said nothing but smiled.

In my dream, I was looking up at her as she stood in a window about four or five floors from the ground. Same dress and pearls. She smiled and waved. I turned to my side to tell someone, probably Bill. When I looked back, she was gone.

The assessment coordinator from Community Care Access Centre and the funeral home prearrangement counsellor arrive within five minutes of each other at about 5:00 p.m. Earlier in the day, when they phoned to set up appointments, I arranged for Sukaine from CCAC to come midafternoon, and then Anne an hour or so later, that being the order of our current priorities. But things are not going as planned today.

The three of us sit at the dining room table and I provide the crib-note version of our past five days. Sukaine has information from the hospital on the diagnosis and Dr. Hii's referral form, but she asks me more about medical history and our domestic situation. She's good. From the discussion, I can see her mind racing systematically through a checklist of Bill's current functional difficulties and the supports that would be most responsive to those needs.

Now she wants to talk to Bill. I take her into the bedroom and nervously wake Bill. I'm relieved when his wakening demeanour gives no hint of this morning's eruption.

"Hey, darling, this is Sukaine. She's from CCAC and is here to assess what homecare help we could use."

"What's your name?" he asks.

"Sukaine, *soo-kine-na*, but don't worry about trying to pronounce it. I know it sounds strange."

"No, I want to know. Sukaine. So you're East Asian?"

"That's right. My family comes from Bangalore, but I've lived here in Canada all my life."

I'm praying that Bill doesn't start speaking in his Indian dialect. Sukaine asks me to leave so that she can talk to Bill alone. I leave the bedroom door slightly ajar. I want to half-eavesdrop while Anne and I go over funeral options. I'm getting practiced at multitasking.

Where Sukaine was all professional efficiency, Anne is sympathetically pastoral. They are well suited to their respective roles. I notice that she has unpacked a big binder and placed a detailed order form on the table. But she pays no attention to them. We just talk about what's been going on with Bill and how I'm coping. I hear some laughter from the bedroom. His and hers. I think that's a good sign.

After about fifteen minutes, Sukaine comes back to the dining room. With apologies to Anne, I turn my attention to her. She shares her analysis, opening with, "Well, this is clearly an urgent situation. He's obviously in considerable discomfort even with the pain medication. He became quite disoriented during our conversation. I'm concerned that he hasn't eaten for over a week. That would of course explain why he is not having any bowel movements. And he is weak." I tell her about his fall yesterday, which I had forgotten to mention earlier. So many things to remember. She excuses herself from the table, pulls out her cell phone, and calls a CCAC supervisor.

I shift my attention to Anne. Feeling task-oriented, I suggest that we talk about specifics. She opens the binder and describes options for ordering a service package or à la carte. My term, not hers.

Sukaine comes back to the table. "I've ordered nursing care services for Bill. CCAC will assign an agency. The situation warrants a daily visit. Is that okay with you?"

"Ah, yeah, that would be good, I guess."

"We'll have to get him transferred."

"Oh no, we want to keep him here at home."

"Sorry, I meant we need to get his doctor to sign over authority of Bill as a patient to one of our palliative care doctors. Yes, everything that we're doing is to arrange it so that he can stay here." Thank God. "What do you think about a hospital bed?" she asks. "There's no room in the bedroom, but he really should be in one. It would make it much safer for him and easier to care for him. Any idea where one could be placed?"

"I can disassemble the sofa and we can have it right here in the living room."

"Good. That will work. Let me call and see how soon we can get one. Probably a commode too." She pulls out her phone and dials again.

"I don't think we'd need all these components of the package outlined here," I say to Anne, picking up the conversation from where we left off.

"Well, maybe not, although I should point out that you do get a substantial discount by buying a package rather than selecting individual components. And there might be services that occur to you later that you'd like to access."

"But if his body is going to be cremated, we wouldn't need 'facility vehicles' as listed here, would we?"

"Actually, that covers the picking up of his body from here once he passes and transferring it to the crematorium. You also mentioned that you would hold a memorial service at your church. There would probably be flowers that would need to be taken to the church from the funeral home after the visitation."

Bill hates the euphemism "passes." I'm glad he's not in the room. He might have used a profanity.

Her sales pitch is softening me and I'm also seeing the merits of not having to worry whether I've paid for something or not. If I choose a package, everything is included. This is my lover, for God's sake. His funeral is my responsibility. I'm not going to nickel and dime it.

Sukaine interrupts. "Okay, it looks like we might be able to get a hospital bed this evening. There is a Medigas truck somewhere in the vicinity. They're trying to contact the driver now. I'm sorry, but I'm going to have to go. I still have another couple of clients to see. I'll leave this binder with you. I've written up my report here. The nurses who come will update it daily. Where would you like it left?"

"Right here on the dining room table is probably best. I think this room is going to be party central."

She looks at me quizzically.

I escort her to the door. "Thank you so very much," I blubber. "This feels tremendously supportive."

We shake hands. "That's our job. I hope things go as well as possible. Under the circumstances."

I sign the contract with Anne. She leaves me with her card and the funeral home phone number to call when it is time to implement the plan. I wonder how long it will be before I make that call.

Bill is sound asleep. I head back to the computer where I compose and send out the following update:

First the good news. The coordinator for Community Care Access Centre has just left and a wonderful support system is being rapidly geared up to help me with many things, from technical medical issues to housekeeping support.

A hospital bed is being brought into the condo tonight.

That will give you a sense of the bad news. Bill's deterioration is like a waterfall. As of this afternoon, according to the CCAC coordinator, there is evidence that the cancer may have metastasized into the brain.

It was just last Friday, August 7, that we got the diagnosis of stage 4 pancreatic cancer—stage 4 meaning it had not only enveloped the pancreas but had spread to other organs, in Bill's case the lungs, liver, and lymph nodes. At that point, other than his being in a wheelchair, he was the same Bill that you all have known and loved. No more. That's only five days ago.

Pray for us.

Love, David

P.S. I just initiated the prearrangement plan with the funeral home this afternoon too—just a bit more evidence of the "bad news."

P.P.S. Our 33rd anniversary is next Monday (August 17)!

Within an hour, a hospital bed is delivered and assembled in our living room.

I have a picture of Bill in a similar-sized but more elegant bed, a berth in our private compartment on the luxury Aurora Express heading from Moscow to St. Petersburg. A glass of tea and a plate of red and black caviar sit on the table beside him. He's holding a book describing the exquisite collection of antique jewelled Fabergé eggs that we had visited the day before in the Kremlin Museum.

One of my talents was planning our vacations.

In September 2002, Bill flew to Moscow to join me at the conclusion of a climate change conference at which I had spoken on environmental ethics on behalf of the World Council of Churches. We spent a few days touring Moscow while staying at the Hotel

Ukraina, one of the "seven sisters" skyscrapers built in the Stalinist architectural style. Then we boarded our train to St. Petersburg. It was raining when the train pulled into the station. No sooner had it come to a halt than our compartment door opened. A gentleman holding a large black umbrella greeted us, ready to usher us to a waiting car that would take us to the elegant, historic Astoria Hotel where I had booked us for five days. Our room looked out onto the illuminated dome of St. Isaac's Cathedral, the largest church in the city. We spent days exploring the Winter Palace of Catherine the Great and the Hermitage, which houses one of the world's largest collections of European art. We saw a performance of *Swan Lake* by the Kirov Ballet at the Mariinsky Theatre. Marina, the aunt of our Stratford neighbour Maureen, acted as gracious host and tour guide to some of the hidden treasures of her native city.

When we got home, Bill bought me an art book with the following inscription:

Thank you for the wonderful trip. I know that you did a phenomenal amount of excellent organisation and spent so much money and effort to make the entire trip an experience of a lifetime—and it was!! This book is just a small thank-you.

Love, Bill

The trip rivalled my 1999 endeavour that took us to Venice, Florence, and Milan for which I got rave reviews from Michelin/Conklin.

It always thrilled me to be able to thrill him.

Chapter Seven—Thursday, August 13

The phone. I answer on the second ring. I want to minimize the possible disruptions to Bill's sleep. Awake, he is in pretty constant pain. Asleep, I assume that he is less conscious and maybe even dreaming something pleasant.

"Hello, is this William Conklin?"

I wince. Better get used to it, I caution myself. Telling callers he is not available will be standard fare.

"I'm sorry, he is not available."

There is a hesitation on the other end of the line before the voice asks, "Is this his caregiver?"

So it's not a marketing call. My attention rivets up multiple levels. "Yes, yes, this is David Hallman, Bill's partner. Who is speaking, please?"

"Hi. My name is Meynardo, the nurse from Saint Elizabeth's Health Care assigned to come to see William. I'm just down the street. Is it convenient for me to come over now?"

"Oh, by all means. Please do." I confirm that he knows the entry code and the condo number. Then I call Rufat, the daytime concierge on the front desk. "Hi, Rufat. This is David in 3109. There is a nurse on his way to see Bill. You can send him right up when he arrives."

"Certainly, David. If there is anything we can do, please let us know."

The staff in our new condo building adores Bill. Huda, the property manager, says that her day is incomplete if she hasn't seen and chatted with Bill. Maggie, her secretary, has already run an errand to pick up a prescription for us. Rufat and the other concierge staff respect Bill so much for the way that he supported them when some scumbag visitors to the building threw racist slurs at them. Johannie and Aron love that he jabbers away to them in their native Spanish. Hakim, the superintendent, has great conversations with Bill about his homeland, Egypt. They all know that Bill has not been well. They'd seen him in the wheelchair during July when we were going to doctors' appointments or to labs. Now, they have heard about Friday's diagnosis, I guess through the building grapevine. Their distress at the news is palpable. I see it in their eyes and hear it in their voices.

Meynardo is a slight man with warm eyes and a quiet manner. I welcome him at the door and lead him into the apartment. "Do you want to see Bill right away?" I ask.

"Not quite yet. I'd like to talk to you to get more background and look at the notes that Sukaine left yesterday. Oh, I see the bed has arrived. That's good."

We sit down at the dining room table. "Yes, it came last evening, but I was nervous about moving him into it on my own. I was hoping that we could do that together?"

"Absolutely. You have a beautiful view from here. Have you lived here long?"

"Not long enough. We just moved in last October, ten months ago. It's a new building and Bill designed a lot of the elements of our suite. We had intended it to be our long-term retirement residence ..." I can't finish the thought.

Meynardo smiles, reaches over, and squeezes my hand. He opens the binder and reads through Sukaine's notes while I gaze out at the view that Bill and I were supposed to enjoy together for years to come.

We go into the bedroom and I rub Bill's arm. "Hey, darling, can you wake up? This is Meynardo, who is going to check in on you each morning." True, I've just woken him, so grogginess is to be expected. But he's not responding and I have to shake him a little more vigorously. Gradually, he opens his eyes and I repeat the introductions.

"Hi, Bill. My name is Meynardo. I'm just going to check your blood pressure and pulse first and then we can chat a bit."

I'm not use to seeing Bill so affectless. Without comment, he lets Meynardo wrap the blood pressure monitor around his arm and then hold his wrist. "How are you feeling this morning, Bill?" Meynardo asks.

"Uh, okay, I guess," he says so softly Meynardo has to ask him to repeat.

"David and I are going to move you into a new bed. We've got a hospital bed set up in the living room that will be safer for you. Are you ready? Can you swing your legs around and put your feet on the floor so we can help you up?"

Bill looks at us but doesn't make a move. I repeat Meynardo's request and take a hold of Bill's legs to shift his body so we can get him up.

"Ow!" he yells. Now he is alert.

"I know that this will be a bit uncomfortable, but it won't take long," I lie.

Meynardo and I assume positions on either side of Bill, take a hold under each arm, and lift him gently.

"Oww. Oww. What are you doing?" he shouts.

"Can you put weight on your legs, Bill, and stand up? We'll hold you tight," Meynardo encourages, not wanting to lose any momentum. It takes a few minutes for Bill to actually place weight on his feet while we struggle to hold him steady. Meynardo nods his head toward the door and we start walking Bill to his new bed. The process takes about five minutes with Bill protesting all the way. Finally, we are able to back him toward the hospital bed and ease his bum down onto the mattress. "Good, good," says Meynardo. "We'll let you rest for a moment, and then we'll swing your legs up onto the bed." Bill moves to accomplish that himself. He has a history of eagerly crawling onto a bed that looks inviting and that offers the potential for rest.

"Attention, passengers on British Airways Flight 92 to London. Attention, please."

Bill and I glanced at each other nervously, hoping we were not going to hear about a delay. We were heading to Grand Bretagne for a week of theatre, opera, and sightseeing over an elongated Easter weekend.

"Unfortunately, this flight has been overbooked. British Airways is seeking volunteers who would be willing to give up their seats on this evening's departure. In exchange, you will be guaranteed a seat on tomorrow's flight and a cash bonus."

In a millisecond, Bill's expression flashed from anxiety to anticipation. My Billy-boy was always game when there was a chance to make a farthing or two. "How about it? Shall we volunteer? Nice to have some extra spending money," he prodded.

"But we've only got a week as it is, minus the travel days," I protested, already preparing myself for inevitable defeat.

"It'll be fine. We haven't scheduled any of our theatre tickets until the beginning of the week anyway."

"Okay. Let's see what they are offering."

Next thing I knew, it was twenty-four hours later and we were in upgraded business-class seats, having been sent home the previous night in a limo, picked up in a limo to be brought back to the airport, and five hundred dollars richer. Bill, wanting to make the most of the perks, was already on his second glass of free champagne and we hadn't even started taxiing onto the runway.

"Excuse me, stewardess, but when do they pull the curtains? My eyes are getting weary having to see the hoi polloi back in steerage." She guffawed most unprofessionally and told him he'd have to suffer until after take-off.

The meal was gourmet, complemented by a variety of wines appropriate to each course, all served on white linen, china, and sterling silver. This was the mid-1980s, after all.

About halfway through the flight, meaning halfway through the truncated night, Bill figured he had better get a bit of sleep. A friend had given him a couple Halcyon sleeping pills (banned several years later) to help during the flight. Unaccustomed to taking any sleeping aids, Bill was surprised when the first one didn't immediately send him off to reverieland. So, of course, he took a second one. Within two minutes he was snoring. Bill had kept the flight crew in stitches for the past couple hours and they were disappointed that their source of boredom relief had been temporarily silenced.

I snoozed for a while until the arrival of breakfast. Bill had made the most of the earlier dinner and was sleeping so soundly that I decided not to waken him. Breakfast came and went and still he slept. The captain's announcement about the beginning of the descent into Heathrow did rouse him. "I've got to go to the bathroom," he said through a groggy haze.

"Okay, but you better make it fast. It won't be long until we are landing," I warned.

Five minutes passed. Ten minutes. Bill was still in the bathroom. Feeling awkward in front of our fellow business-class passengers, I nevertheless approached the bathroom and tapped lightly on the door. "Bill, you'd better return to your seat." No answer.

"Is there a problem?" the flight attendant asked.

"My partner is in the bathroom."

"Well, he should be in his seat by now."

"Exactly. That's what I'm trying to tell him, but I can't get any response."

She knocked on the door. "Sir, you have to return to your seat. We've begun our descent." No response. Harder knocking. "Sir, can you hear me? You have to be seated." Nothing. She motioned to her male colleague who came over and ever more forcefully knocked on the door, repeating the same message. He tried opening the door. Of course, it was locked from the inside. He pulled out a pen, jammed it into the door handle, trying to force it open, and in the process broke part of the opening mechanism. I glanced at the window and we were clearly approaching terra firma.

Suddenly, the door opened and Bill, looking rather miffed, asked what the racket was about. I ushered him unceremoniously back to our seats and buckled him in, whereupon he promptly fell sound asleep again. It was at that point that I put two and two together. Sleeping pills on top of multiple glasses of champagne, wine, and an after-dinner liqueur likely explained his virtually comatose state.

Once landed, we let all the other passengers exit and they brought a wheelchair. The BA staff was worried that he might be seriously ill. I was too embarrassed to share my theory. They directed us toward the infirmary on the arrivals level. While trying to keep him from toppling over in the wheelchair, I searched for our bags at the carousel only to discover a pair of look-a-likes, but not ours. Someone had taken the wrong bags. I went over to the lost luggage counter, somnambulant lover in tow, to fill out the requisite forms. Having completed the paperwork, I looked once more at the carousel and saw that ours had been returned. I loaded them on a luggage cart and manoeuvred cart and wheelchair toward the infirmary door. As the intake officer interviewed me, Bill came temporarily to consciousness and eyed a lovely-looking gurney on which he could stretch out rather than doze uncomfortably in the wheelchair. After panicking for a moment when I noticed the empty wheelchair, I saw him sound asleep on the gurney. An attendant wheeled the bed into a private room where he continued his peaceful rest for the next eight hours. Periodically, while sleeping beauty was out of it, I called our guest house begging them not to release our reservation. Eventually, about 4:00 p.m. in the afternoon, he woke up quite oblivious to where we were and why.

"Hello, sir," said the nurse. "How are you feeling? Can I get you anything?"

"Oh, a cup of tea would be lovely," Bill replied. He turned to me and said, "This is such a civilised country."

I suspect that BA put us on their no-fly list.

Bill is surrounded by memorabilia of our life together.

Above the headboard of the hospital bed hangs our signed Dali etching, *Coronation in Venice*. We bought it in 1981 at an auction in support of mental health. Venice is one of our favourite cities. We have sat enjoying many an espresso in Piazza San Marco depicted in the picture.

Over Bill's left shoulder is mounted the Egyptian sarcophagus head that we bought at the Art Gallery of Ontario. In 1979, Bill and I, as members of the AGO, were able to tour the original King Tut exhibition on the first day. As we came out of the exhibition and into the gift shop, Bill spotted right away the antique sarcophagus head. The Egyptian government had sent about a half-dozen antiquities to each of the museums hosting the King Tut exhibit, which those museums could sell. We looked at the mask and Bill said to the clerk "Okay." I thought he meant, "Okay, thank you for showing it to us." What he meant was, "Okay, we'll take it." It has hung on the living room wall in our various homes ever since. As a follow-up to the visit, we took advantage of an AGO tour to Egypt in June 1980. We spent ten glorious days in Cairo, Luxor, and the Valley of the Kings and then a week in Paris on our way home. The mask evokes those wonderful memories for me every time I look at it.

To Bill's right sits our black ebony baby grand piano. In March 2006, when we were looking at the floor plans of the various suites to be built in a new Tridel development called Verve, the perky salesperson came over to us, directed us to the 2D+D suite (which Bill always joked stood for two dormitories), and said, "This is the model that you will want." We studied its unique layout and Bill asked, "But what would one do with this area where the living room comes to a point?"

"Oh, that is where you would put your grand piano, darling," she replied without losing a beat. Bill and I looked at each other aghast and then turned to this stranger.

Bill said something to the effect of, "Are you psychic or maybe a witch? We'll take it."

I added, "On the highest floor available." Teresa, the salesperson, became one of our dearest friends at that instant and remains so.

Beyond the piano and all across the south side of Bill's thirty-first-floor hospital room stretch panoramic windows. If he opens his eyes, he would see Toronto's skyline, the Toronto Islands, Lake Ontario, and, on a clear day, the towers of Niagara Falls across the lake. This stunning vista has been one of the joys for us of the new condo.

But Bill is not opening his eyes. He's sleeping almost continuously.

Chapter Eight—Friday, August 14

Most mornings since Bill's diagnosis a week ago, he has chosen one of his favourite hymns to sing and I have accompanied him on the piano, softly so as not to drown him out. Today, he selects "Breath on Me, Breath of God." That vibrant tenor voice that used to demonstrate vocal technique for his students, navigate the complexities of operatic arias, and lead group carols at Christmas, now struggles to get through the two-line hymn. We finish and he closes his eyes to rest and recover from this morning's effort. I suspect that this may have been the last of such devotionals.

When Meynardo arrives and checks Bill's blood pressure and pulse, both are still within the normal range. That seems incongruous to me. My lover lies largely unresponsive in this hospital bed in our living room sometimes in an almost semicomatose state and yet these physiological readings are "normal."

We are sitting at the dining room table and as Meynardo opens the binder to write up his daily progress notes, he hesitates and then asks, "Have you thought about what you would need to do if Bill dies over the weekend?"

So, despite the normal readings, I guess he thinks that Bill's end could be close.

"Well, the funeral home director told me about calling 911."

"Did you and Bill ever have any discussion about DNR?"

"You mean, do not resuscitate? Well, not explicitly, but let me get the power of attorney because I think it says something about that." I retrieve it from the filing cabinet in the library, study it, and find the reference … *should I have an incurable injury, disease, or illness regarded as terminal …*

"What do you think would be Bill's wishes? And yours?"

"Oh, he's ready to die, anxious even. We've had very specific discussions about that, while he was still more conversant, that is."

"Well, as it stands at this point, if he were to die soon, you would be obligated to call 911. The paramedics and firefighters who would arrive would likely feel bound to try and revive him by any means, including CPR. The power of attorney helps express Bill's wishes but they are sometimes reluctant to abide by it if it is old and this one is dated 1997. "

"Oh, God. Bill would not want that." My mind flashes back to his fury about my "reviving" him with a hug and tears the other morning.

"I don't see a copy of the standard DNR form in the binder here. I'll make sure to bring one with me tomorrow morning. You can sign it and that will ensure that Bill's wishes are respected."

Cemeteries and gravesites. Not what one would expect to be high on a tourist's itinerary. But Bill and I always leaned a bit toward the eccentric in our travel curiosities.

A foggy day in London town. We made our way through a labyrinth of paths in Brompton Cemetery trying to decipher the markings on the deteriorating headstones. Eventually, we found the large marble slab covering the final resting place of Austrian-born tenor Richard Tauber. Bill was a fan of his old recordings. Tauber made his last stage appearance as Ottavio in *Don Giovanni*, performed at Covent Garden on September 27, 1947. He had been fighting a battle with cancer for quite some time. During this final performance, his left lung was nearly consumed by cancer, but this did not stop him from giving a stunning performance. His gravestone includes the following epitaph by A. P. Herbert: *A golden singer with a sunny heart, the heart's delight of millions was his art, now that rich roaring tender voice beguiles, attentive angels in the land of smiles.* Two days after paying our respects to Tauber, we spent the evening of Valentine's Day (Friday, February 14, 1992) at the Royal Opera House in Covent Garden listening to a performance of *Don Giovanni.*

Once we lost and refound our way several times, Eva Peron's tomb appeared rather modest in comparison to many of the grand mausoleums that we had passed. Recoleta Cemetery in one of Buenos Aires' trendiest neighbourhoods houses the remains of many of the rich and powerful who ruled and brought so much grief to Argentina's people. We weren't sure if we were paying respects to the myth or the reality of the great Eva. In any case, I snapped a picture as Bill placed a rose.

November 1995 was cold and rainy and it took a long bus ride for us to reach the Berlin-Schöneberg Cemetery. A bed of pansies, appropriately, adorned the small garden in front of the gravestone of Marlene Dietrich, who rated near the top in Bill's list of gay icons. Every time Bill made a pot of coffee in our house using the porcelain Melita pot and filter, he insisted on referring to it as Frau Bertholt coffee and mimicked Dietrich's graceful hospitality as she poured a cup for Burt Lancaster in the 1961 classic, *Judgment at Nuremburg.* Then there were Bill's renditions of some of Marlene's biggest hits sung with German accent and double entendre: "Just a Gigolo," "The Boys in the Back Room," and "Falling in Love Again." How could we not pay homage to the grand Marlene if we were in Berlin?

One can't mention gay icons without including Oscar Wilde. With Bill's fine taste in design, he appreciated Wilde's final words before death as he gazed around the decrepit Parisian apartment that had become his home after his exile from England: "Either that wallpaper goes, or I do." The day we made our way to Paris's Cimetière Père Lachaise to pay our respects in June 1980, there was a steady stream of visitors, most of whom, like us, probably said a quiet prayer of gratitude for one who had borne so much.

This afternoon we have the first visit from Tiblez of Toronto Homemakers Service. She helps me replace the bedding with clean linens and change Bill, and she gives him a sponge bath. I attempt to shave him, not very successfully. It's all done in the hospital bed; Bill has not had the strength to get out of bed since Meynardo and I first moved him into it two days ago.

I don't know if people are born with the disposition for this kind of work or if they just get such good training. Tiblez is a natural at it and a godsend for me. I love her.

Bill is not so keen. Not that he has anything against her personally. He seems hardly cognizant of whose hands are touching his body. What he does experience is our moving him from side to side as we change him and the bedding. He cries out in pain. I try to console him with platitudes. Short-term pain for a little longer-term gain. Easy for me to say.

I don't understand well how the system works. It feels like magic. Meynardo makes a few calls when he is here in the mornings and suddenly there is Saint Tiblez at my door a few hours later. Deliveries from the pharmacy come regularly. Our walk-in closet assumes the role of ad hoc repository for the boxes of incontinence briefs, absorption pads for the bed, mouth swabs, latex gloves, and hand sanitizers. Medications come by special delivery.

Rufat and the other concierge staff don't disturb me by calling to announce the arrival of another helper or delivery. They just send them up. How quickly our new routine, our new life, has become established.

Before we met, Bill spent time on the other side of the health care recipient/provider table. For several years, to make money during university, he had summer and part-time winter jobs working as an emergency room orderly, including some shifts in the fracture clinic. He got to do a wide range of procedures. He used to love describing them to me in great detail knowing my queasiness in relation to anything having to do with pain, spurting blood, protruding bones, or exposed internal organs.

His place of employment was the old Wellesley Hospital. It was closed in 1998 as part of a restructuring process of health care facilities in Toronto. The buildings were torn down and the site sold. A developer later bought part of the site and eventually erected a modern condo complex called Verve.

Bill's aunt Marion, his father's sister, comes down from Sutton for a visit this afternoon, driven into Toronto by a friend more accustomed to city traffic than she. Mame, as Bill affectionately called her over the years, sent a letter earlier this week:

My heart is just aching over your diagnosis. I am so sorry. The only comfort I have is your relationship with God. You have never doubted his love for you or that he walks with you at all times ...

Mame arrives with a bouquet of roses and a card addressed to both Bill and me for our anniversary coming up next week. She is the only family member to acknowledge it.

I wake Bill and tell him that Aunt Mame is here to visit him. He opens his eyes as she leans over the bed rail and kisses his forehead. He looks directly at her and seems to smile. She sits by his bed holding his hand, reminiscing about years gone by, thanking him for his concern for her over the years, and laughing about their many phone conversations.

Blinking tears from her eyes, she turns to me. "You know my friends were so impressed that Billy used to call me all the way from Mexico when you boys were down there in February each year. And last October, when there was all the publicity about the economic crisis, he phoned and told me not to worry, everything would work out all right. He even asked me if I needed any financial assistance, which I didn't, of course, because of my pension. My best friend was so jealous because she said that her own son didn't show as much concern about her as my nephew showed me."

Turning back to Bill she says, "Well, little Billy, I shouldn't overstay my welcome. I can tell you are tired. Just remember that I love you so much and I'll be praying for you."

I'm grateful that she's family. To me as well as to Bill.

Bill was an only child. My two brothers have lived most of their lives in the United States. This meant that Bill and I were the primary caregivers for both sets of parents as they aged. We did a lot of work caring for them, but we also had many wonderful times together as a family.

For quite a few years, we treated our parents to one of the musical productions at the Stratford Festival, scheduling it around the end of May to coincide with Bill's mom's birthday. The final time that we were able to organise it with my parents was 2003. The musical was *The King and I*. The production of our family adventure was almost as complex as the performance on stage. Mom's mobility had deteriorated to the point that she was permanently wheelchair-bound. Dad's dementia was starting to take hold. We arranged for an accessible taxi-service to pick them up at their apartment in Waterloo and bring them to our home in Stratford. There we had a light lunch and then Bill and his mom headed over to the theatre by taxi in order to be there to meet the rest of us. I chauffeured my parents and the wheelchair in our car. Before entering the theatre, I had a passerby take a picture of the five of us—a treasured memento of a last time family outing. We had booked two seats in the accessible section of the theatre for Mom and Dad. Bill, Adelle, and I sat together further down in the orchestra. At intermission, I scooted back to where Mom and Dad were sitting to see how they were doing. Mom was pretty exhausted. It had been a long day for her already. Dad, through his increasing blurred perceptions, gestured toward the stage and asked somewhat indignantly, "What's all the kerfuffle going on down there? Noise and lights and people running all around!" I almost laughed out loud. It was a review that the director would not have appreciated, but it was my dad. I decided that they had had enough cultural experience for the day. I called the taxi company to revise the prearranged pick-up time and the three of us waited for it in the warm May sun sitting by the gardens that surround the theatre.

Later, Bill gave me his commentary of the second half of the play that I had missed. He was a little more generous than Dad had been.

Huda calls from the management office downstairs and asks if it would be possible for her and some of the staff to come up and say hello to Bill. What she is really talking about is saying good-bye to Bill, but I know that that is too painful a truism for her to speak.

I greet them at the door—Huda, Maggie, Rufat, Hakim, Johannie, and Aron. They are all so respectful and quietly dignified, as befits the visit. I bring them into the living room and they gather around Bill's bed. I can discern a few sharp intakes of breath among them on seeing Bill.

"Bill, you have some visitors," I say softly as I rub his arm, trying to rouse him. The head of the bed is always slightly raised to protect his respiratory system so when he opens his eyes, they are all directly in his line of sight.

"Hi, Bill," Huda says, assuming her role as manager. "We've come to bring our greetings. We miss seeing you around the building."

Bill's eyes open double their usual size and a huge grin takes hold of his face. With a clarity of voice that I haven't heard in days, he declares, "Oh, you people. I love you all. You've made our home such a wonderful place to live."

All of us gathered around the bed are stunned and in tears.

Chapter Nine—Saturday, August 15

I'm sitting in the chair beside Bill's bed wincing at his coughing, which sounds so uncomfortable. No, coughing isn't the right word. It's like a violent hiccup mixed with a gagging. It goes on for over a half hour at a time, more so at night than during the daytime, it seems. I would assume it is keeping Bill awake, but it is hard to tell. His eyes are closed and he is generally less responsive all the time. And what would be the use asking him about it anyway? Obviously, it is causing him distress. I can tell that by his furrowed brow.

It is now 3:00 a.m. and these periodic bouts have been occurring on a regular basis for the past several hours. I add it to my list of things to report to Meynardo in the morning.

I've got to get some sleep. I am so exhausted. Hot chocolate might knock me out for a while. I boil water and make myself a cup. I step out onto the balcony to sit and drink it on this warm summer night.

Carnation used to be the hot chocolate brand of choice in our household until the company was bought by Nestlé. No product by Nestlé or any of its multitudinous subsidiaries has crossed our threshold in thirty years. Bill saw to that.

From 1979 until 1984, I was the coordinator of the Nestlé boycott for The United Church of Canada and by extension one of the organisers of the Canadian campaign. I also acted as secretary for the International Nestlé Boycott Committee (INBC). A number of large multinational infant formula manufacturers were using aggressive marketing tactics to persuade mothers in developing countries to opt for formula rather than breastfeed. Many infants were getting sick because of the lack of clean water to mix with the formula. This, combined with missing out on the natural immunities conferred on a baby through breast milk, resulted in the incidence of morbidity and mortality throughout poor countries being much higher for bottle-fed infants than breast-fed ones. Nestlé was one of the most egregious offenders with slick campaigns painting formula as the modern way and inducing health care workers to promote it with free gifts. The company representatives would distribute just enough free samples to new mothers to use until they were no longer lactating, at which point they would have no option but to spend high proportions of the scarce family income for more formula. In 1984, we spent days in acrimonious face-to-face negotiations with the company at UNICEF headquarters in New York. Nestlé finally conceded to our demands to terminate all such unethical marketing schemes. The INBC agreed to the call off the boycott.

During the years that I was the Nestlé Boycott Campaign coordinator, Bill was a self-appointed enforcer, the muscle, a capo. He distributed boycott literature to all our family and friends, and threatened them with excommunication if they did not comply. He posted pamphlets on every store bulletin board he could find, always carrying a supply so that he could put up another copy as soon as he noticed the store manager had taken down the initial one. He regularly phoned Nestlé corporate offices and regaled them about their scuzzy practices and lack of ethics.

That's my Billy-boy.

Bill is not very responsive and his breathing is noticeably shallower during Meynardo's visit. I ask him if he thinks that's significant. He describes some of the varieties of breathing patterns that people go through during their final stages but cautions me that that doesn't mean that anything is imminent. Bill could survive in this state for quite a long time.

Is that good news or not?

My mind has been off wandering somewhere when I realise that Meynardo has finished his note writing and is sitting looking at me. "How are you doing?" he asks.

"Oh, I'm okay I guess. A little tired and stressed, but that's no surprise."

"Are you sleeping much?"

"No, not really."

"What if we had someone come in to sit with Bill overnight so you could get some decent sleep?"

"That would be possible?" I ask incredulously.

"Yes. Currently, you're only using two hours. That's for the personal support worker who comes in to help you bathe Bill. Your situation here justifies much more than that."

He gets on the phone and starts the ball rolling for a PSW to come overnight as of tonight. I'm amazed at how efficiently and rapidly this whole health care support system has been mobilised for us.

"So what do you do?" I could tell it was a classic medical strategy on his part to divert my attention from the needle and stitches that he had poised ready to insert into my bleeding hand.

"I'm sort of a writer, I guess," I said staring at the chart of the circulatory system hanging on the wall, determined to look at anything other than the real-life blood.

"Oh yeah, what do you write?"

"Well, I work for The United Church of Canada on environmental issues. I do educational work and coordinate advocacy. I've written a few books on environmental ethics." The local anaesthetic dulled any pain, but my peripheral vision caught the up-and-down motion of his fingers. I closed my eyes.

"I'm doing some writing too," he said.

"Medical textbooks?"

"No. Fiction, actually. I'm writing a novel. It's based on my experiences as an emergency room doctor."

"No kidding." I'm intrigued. Successfully distracted from the procedure at hand, I reopened my eyes as we continued the conversation about the joys and challenges of writing.

Fifteen minutes later, I'm repaired and ready to face the world again. "When do you expect to finish the novel? And what's your name by the way?"

"Oh, it will still be a while. I don't have a lot of free time with my shifts here at the hospital. Vincent Lam is my name."

In 2006, Dr. Vincent Lam won the Scotiabank Giller Prize for his novel *Bloodletting & Miraculous Cures*.

The next time I was in that emergency room at Toronto East General Hospital was on August 7, 2009, ten years after my cut hand incident. This time Bill was the patient.

Bill's cousin Leslie and her son James arrive from Keswick. I try to rouse Bill but to no avail. Yesterday, at least he opened his eyes and seemed to recognise his aunt Mame. I can tell it is deeply dispiriting for Leslie to see Bill like this. Bill has been a great support to her as she has gone through some health problems. They used to talk on the phone frequently.

After they leave, I prepare and send out another update.

Dear family and friends,

The slowing-down process continues. Bill is sleeping much of the time, which I have thought of as a good thing. But yesterday, and even more so today, when a couple family members came to visit him, it was very difficult to get him to open his eyes at all and acknowledge them. He appeared to be almost in a semicomatose state. It is very hard to hear anything he says because he speaks so softly—he now lacks the lung capacity to project. This is extremely frustrating to him. He seems to be more restless and in greater distress during the nights than during the daytime. He has long spells at night (thirty to forty minutes) of something that seems an amalgam of a cough, a hack, and a hiccup. The nurse, during his daily visit this morning, said that with the lungs being one of the organs into which the cancer has metastasized, there may be fluids being produced that Bill's body is trying to expectorate. It is clearly uncomfortable for him and keeps him awake at night. Though many aspects of his body are weakening, his heart keeps functioning and his blood pressure is apparently in the normal range. That suggests that the heart is not about to give out in the immediate future—something that Bill does not view as a blessing in this context.

The nurse this morning also expressed concern about my apparent fatigue. He got on the phone right away and so as of tonight from 11:00 p.m. until 7:00 a.m. tomorrow, we'll have a PSW (personal support worker) staying in the living room where we have set up the hospital bed to watch Bill and attend to him, while I sleep in the bedroom. This will allow me to hopefully get a good night's sleep for the first time in ten days. This is in addition to the PSW who comes for two hours during the day to help me bathe him in *bed, change his clothing and bed linens, etc. That's been an enormous help because they have skills in carrying for a bedridden person that I don't. This cleaning/hygiene routine, though, is very distressing to Bill because of the need to move him from side to side in the bed, which is painful for him, and to wash his increasingly thin and sensitive skin. The Community Care Access Centre (CCAC) had two boxes of supplies delivered to us yesterday including incontinence briefs, mouth cleaners, sterilising soap, etc.---the sort of things one would find in a hospital. On Monday, we'll be visited by the principle CCAC palliative care doctor. All of this, the personnel and the material goods, are provided to us at no charge through the health care system. The amount of home care available to persons in our situation has been a revelation to me.*

Then there are the many friends in our building (including building management staff) and around the neighbourhood who have been running errands for me, picking up medication and groceries, giving me an extra pair of arms at night when I need to move Bill in his bed, etc. I'm immensely grateful to them.

You have all been so generous in your messages of support. Thank you for walking with us on this day-by-day journey.

Love, David

P.S. Bill would be furious if he knew that I was telling you all this stuff. But I write because I know that you love him and want to know what is happening, and because in my own fragile emotional state, I need to share it and experience your support in return.

Valerie knocks on the door at 10:55 p.m. I open the door and she takes Bill into her care for the night and both of us into her heart. She's quiet, efficient, empathetic, and maternal.

I get a solid night's sleep for the first time in weeks.

Chapter Ten—Sunday, August 16

Bill gives yes/no answers to Meynardo's questions this morning, which means that he is more alert than he was yesterday. Meynardo makes the good suggestion that I should time the giving of painkillers to Bill so that they kick in just before we have to move him to change him or the bedding. Shifting Bill around in the bed is so distressing for him and his cries indicate how excruciating the pain must be. I castigate myself for not having thought of Meynardo's strategy days ago.

After Meynardo's visit, I spend some time reading the e-mail responses that have come in from family and friends since last evening's update. This technology is a lifesaver for me, or at least for my sanity. The communications are full of love, concern, and support. Our friends are sojourning with Bill and me through these unbelievable days. They appreciate being invited along. I am immensely grateful for their company.

Each year that we went to Puerto Vallarta and stayed at Susan's place, Snake adopted us for the duration of our stay.

The first year, we were just unpacking our bags and in he sauntered, jumped up on the bed, made himself at home, and stayed in our unit almost continuously for the month. Snake is an orange tabby cat just like our Simon at home. So it has been wonderful for us to have a Simon surrogate during vacation periods in PV every February.

Snake sends his love each time that Susan e-mails or phones to check in on Bill.

The phone rings. A deep baritone voice greets me with, "Hello, darling, how are you doing?" I instantly recognise it as belonging to Walter Borden, an actor with whom we had become good friends during his years at the Stratford Festival.

"Oh, Walter, how good of you to call. You've seen the e-mail message that I sent out about Bill?"

"Yes. I am so very, very sorry. I was wondering if it would be possible for me to come for a quick visit."

"Sure, that would be okay. I should warn you that it's touch and go whether Bill will be awake, or whether there would be any indication that he recognises you."

"That's okay. I'd just like to see him. And you. When would be convenient?"

"The nurse who comes to help me bathe him will be here from about 11 to 1. Could you come maybe about 1:30?"

Walter is at the door promptly at 1:30. He gives me a big bear hug and then sits by Bill's bed, silently stroking his hand for about a half hour. I pull a chair up to sit beside him so we can speak quietly. "Walter, I've started planning for Bill's memorial service and I'm wondering if you would be willing to do a reading or something."

"I would be honoured. Did you have something specific in mind?"

"No. I haven't gotten that far yet. I'm open to suggestions."

"I have the perfect piece. It's from a play of Negro Sermons called *God's Trombones* written by James Weldon Johnson sometime in the 1920s. I've performed it several times, including on CBC. There's one part called 'Go Down Death.'" In hushed tones, but with the emotive eloquence that we so admired on the stage, he recites, "Weep not, weep not, she is not dead; she's resting in the bosom of Jesus. Heartbroken husband, weep no more; grief-stricken son, weep no more; left-lonesome daughter, weep no more; she's only just gone home …"

I hope that Bill is listening.

About five years ago, Bill got a great idea for a play. He said that the two of us should collaborate on writing it. He called it *The Veranda*. His inspiration was the years of conversations and storytelling that took place during the summer months when we pretty much lived on the front veranda of our house in Stratford. Because we were located so centrally in the downtown core, many people, including members of the acting company, would walk by the house on their way to one of the four theatres. Often people stopped to comment on what a beautifully charming house it was. A big part of that appearance was Bill's resurrection of it.

The house was very shabby-looking when we first saw it in 1991, but the "bones" were good. It had been built in 1877 and was of the Italianate Renaissance Revival style. Of course, Bill would know that. I certainly didn't. I wasn't the least bit interested in it when the real estate agent took us through it. Bill, on the other hand, had a vision and was enthused.

He said, "Look at the beautiful mouldings and the marble fireplace and the height of the ceilings." He walked through each room, describing how it could be restored to its former glory and how we could refashion some of the layout to make room for our grand piano, our library, and our antique furniture. Then there was the veranda, which had been made over in a poor 1950s' version of brick modern but which he said could be restored with the right spindles, pillars, and corner brackets.

So he transformed 75 Nile Street into a beautiful home for us where we spent every summer, every Christmas, and many weekends from 1992 until 2009, and on the veranda of which we passed countless hours in conversation with neighbours, friends, actors, festival staff, and complete strangers. So many stories were told on that veranda, some hilarious, others poignant. The stories and the characters who told them would have made for a great play.

Now, the chance for that collaboration between Bill and me is gone.

Late afternoon, there is a knock on the door. I answer it to find Rob and Marco standing, loaded with a freshly cooked, full-course dinner wrapped in towels to keep it all warm.

Before I can even say hello, Rob explains, "We didn't phone to ask you if you wanted anything because we thought you'd probably say you were okay. But we suspect that you haven't been eating, so here we are and you're going to eat." With that they brush past me and into the kitchen to put their repast on the countertop. I'm grateful that they have moved in so officiously. It gave me the chance to wipe away my tears of surprise and gratitude before joining them in the kitchen.

After hugs all round, Marco says, "We're just here for a short visit. We don't want to impose, and we know that you want to keep things as quiet as possible for Bill." I appreciate their sensitivity.

We move over to the bed, and they spend a few minutes gazing quietly at my sleeping lover. "Rob, would you mind saying a prayer?" I ask.

"Of course." The three of us grasp hands. I place one of mine on Bill's arm. Rob does likewise on his other and then asks God's blessing on Bill and me during this time of trial.

We move into the library so we can have more of a conversation without disturbing Bill. Rob and I have known each other for twenty-five years or more through our work for the United Church. Now that I am retired and he is a member of parliament, our paths haven't been crossing as frequently. But he and Marco have been very supportive as I have been caring for Bill during his illness. Just before leaving, Rob, who has known me virtually all my career, says something that startles me. "You know, what you are doing in these days may be the most important work that you have ever done. And that's saying something."

After I close the door, I reflect on his comment. Perhaps the energy and spirit that I brought to my work over the years being involved in macro issues of social, economic, and ecological justice is the same energy and spirit that now infuses me on the micro level of relationship with my dying partner and the palliative caregiving for other family members who died over the past few years. I'm grateful for this new perspective.

During my career, I worked mainly at analysis and strategy on systemic issues such as climate change and global ethics. I hope it made a difference.

During his life, Bill worked mainly at the level of individuals through his teaching and his befriending of persons in need. He changed lives.

It is a quiet Sunday evening in suite 3109, the atmosphere cuddled by the sweet voices of RyanDan.

One of the preconstruction additions that we arranged for our condo was to have wiring run through the suite so that we could have ceiling mounted speakers in each room. Hearing is the sense that apparently outlasts all others. As Bill has been fading, I have had the sound system tuned mainly to the Baroque or the chamber music station. Sometimes, I put on one of his favourite CDs: Ben Heppner or Sarah Vaughan, Cecilia Bartoli or Keely Smith, Jessye Norman or Etta James, Glenn Gould or Dinah Washington.

I sit beside Bill's bed and moisten his lips. He has not been able to eat anything for over a week. He had been drinking juice a few days ago but now can only handle water. We had been using a straw, but the sucking reflex has diminished. It is a delicate task to prop him up and pour water a bit at a time into his mouth. Too much and he risks choking. Too slowly and he becomes fatigued in the upright position. His painkillers have to be crushed and dissolved in water. It's hard for him to swallow them whole. He is increasingly dehydrated. The use of the mouth swabs help moisturise his chapped lips somewhat.

He has a small framed drawing of Jesus that he loves. Over the past weeks, while confined to bed, he has kept it on a table beside his bed. He would look at it and quietly recite Bible verses: *Be still and know that I am God ... Lo, I am with you always ... Be not troubled, be not afraid ...* Since his diagnosis, I have kept a small candle lit beside the picture at all times. I light a fresh one now and stretch out in the chair opposite the bed.

Chapter Eleven – Monday, August 17

It has been a difficult night for Bill with the coughing spells, but he seems to be sleeping this morning as I approach the bed. I give him a kiss on the forehead. "Happy anniversary, darling." No response.

I hate to disturb him, but we need to change him before Valerie finishes her shift at 7:00 a.m. It's a quicker and easier process if there are two of us. No less painful for Bill though. He opens his eyes and utters a moan as we begin. He cries out as we turn him on his side. For the first time, I notice how red and chapped the skin on his back and buttocks has become. My God, that must be uncomfortable. I mention this in a later conversation with our friend Teresa and she immediately materialises with some hypoallergenic, perfume-free, lanolin-free, nongreasy, moisturizing cream for sensitive skin. She knows about Bill's allergies. She restocks my supply as needed. Bill virtually purrs when we apply it several times a day.

Bill had proposed that we meet at the theatre. I got there early, very early. About fifteen minutes before the performance was scheduled to start, I saw him round the corner. The sight of him gave me goose bumps.

But he was not alone. *What's this about?* He gave me a peck on the cheek and then introduced his friend. I tried to act nonchalant but was majorly disappointed. I thought that this was going to be a romantic first date. Just the two of us. Later in the evening, he confided that he was so nervous about going out with me for the first time that he brought his friend for moral support. That made it forgivable and made him even more endearing in my eyes.

He had chosen the play because he thought from the title it was going to be an avant-garde gay production, something to impress his new boyfriend who apparently liked to jet off to New York on weekends. But *Body Politic* turned out not to be based on the gay newspaper of that name, as Bill had assumed. Rather it was a comedy about the "body politic" in the original sense of the phrase. I confess that I don't remember anything about the production. I was too fixated on the moments when his knee brushed mine or when I could hear the sound of his laughter.

After the play, he was feeling more relaxed and dispatched his friend, the same "friend" who several days later would traumatise Bill with the fiction about my Québecois lover. Bill and I headed to a local gay bar for a drink. We talked nonstop. We ran into someone with whom I volunteered on the gay distress phone line. I was bursting with pride as I introduced Bill to him.

After a beer he said that he would drive me home. I started laughing as we approached his car and explained that we had exactly the same kind of car, a Toyota Celica. Somewhat presumptuously (but wanting my cards clearly on the table), I declared that this must be a sign that we were meant to be together.

He said, "That's right."

I beamed.

He asked, "Is yours paid for, like mine is?"

I cringed.

At the entrance to my apartment building, he gave me a properly chaste good-night kiss. A first-date kiss. He was going to a performance of *Midsummer Night's Dream* in Stratford the next day, but we agreed that we would see each other again the following day.

So ended our first date on August 17, 1976, which we commemorated as our anniversary every year thereafter.

After Meynardo's morning check-up and Tiblez's ever-so-sensitive daily bathing of Bill, I return to my computer in the library. As always, there are new messages to read from friends. I can feel their arms reaching out through the screen and hugging me.

I also have been spending time at my laptop preparing an outline for Bill's memorial service. It is surreal. I am going through the motions, but I don't really believe I am doing this. I want to have lots of music. I have been in touch with Elaine Overholt, a professional musician friend whom Bill and I first met in 1976 within the first month of starting to live together in my apartment. She has agreed to perform at the service. I call her to talk about options for what she might sing. I hold up the phone to Bill's ear and Elaine speaks to him, telling him what an incredible impact he has had on so many people's lives, and how much she loves him. He has pretty much lost his capacity to speak, so he is not able to reply, but it is clear from his eyes and from his expression that he knows who she is and understands what she is saying. She sings a few notes to him of something and then says to him, "Bill, I'm going to sing you up to heaven!" His face is glowing. It is such a gift to see him smiling.

A little later, Chrissie and David come in for a brief visit. They try and keep up a brave face talking to Bill about all the wonderful times that we have had together in Puerto Vallarta. It is hard to tell if he is awake or not. Often, when I would come into the house and hear Bill chortling away on the phone, it was Chrissie whom he was talking to. They had a pattern of savagely insulting each other, and then dissolving in gales of laughter. I know that Chrissie will miss him dearly.

The first year we went to Puerto Vallarta, probably in 1996, Bill brought along a bag full of Valentine's decorations. February 14 fell during our vacation. Early in the morning, we decorated our palapa on the beach with red streamers, balloons, paper hearts, sparkly beads, anything that we had been able to find at the dollar store in Toronto that evoked Valentine's Day, whether tacky or chic. As well, we had bags of mints and candies with "Be My Valentine" stamped on them. About noon, I went off to the bakery and picked up the big tres leches cake that we had ordered the day before. Shortly after I got back to the beach, I received a bouquet of roses by delivery, which Bill had surreptitiously arranged. The day was filled with hilarity as old friends and freshly made ones stopped by to compliment us on our decorations and get a free candy or piece of cake. The Mexican children on the beach were fascinated by the festivities and Bill jabbered away to them in Spanish as he gave them red and white pencils.

The next day was much quieter under our palapa as we recovered not only from the daytime party but the Valentine's celebrations that went on late into the night at the Kit Kat Club, the premier gay martini bar of the time.

"What are we, chopped liver?"

We looked in the direction of the question that had been hurled at us in a heavy Scottish brogue. At the palapa to our right glowered a little mite of a woman.

"My husband and I sat here all day watching all the comings and goings at your party and never once did you glance over and offer us any of the goodies." We apologised profusely and promptly became great friends with Chrissie and David, who we learned were also from Toronto. Every year thereafter we would socialise with them while we were in PV at the same time in February. We would go out for dinner together at other times of the year in Toronto. But most importantly, for both Bill and Chrissie, the two of them would talk almost daily on the phone, a thing of the past now.

I have reconnected over the past year with Gail, a friend from graduate school, lo so many decades ago. She and I were among a group of grad students at Wilfrid Laurier University in Waterloo who were privileged to be part of an innovative programme called Community Psychology, initiated by a new professor at WLU. Gail and Ed, the prof, have been very supportive of Bill and me during this current crisis.

Gail e-mails from work and suggests that she could pick up dinner supplies and bring them over. I respond affirmatively and appreciatively.

We sit at the dining room table devouring her Whole Foods purchases, everything delicious and nutritious. We keep our conversational voices low so as not to disturb Bill asleep in the bed ten feet away.

I rattle on to her about the following:

- Meynardo's daily nursing visits when he checks Bill's vital signs. Though Bill's communication capacity has almost disappeared, his intake of food is long gone, and his fluids consumption is rapidly diminishing, still his blood pressure and pulse remain in the normal range, which means that his heart doesn't appear ready to give up any time soon despite his history of heart problems;

- Tiblez's quiet and sympathetic sponge bathing, teeth brushing, tongue cleaning, pad changing, and gentle application of Teresa's magic moisturizing cream to Bill's desiccated skin;

- Valerie's reassuring nightly presence that is allowing me to get decent sleep for the first time in weeks. I'm frankly surprised at the speed and ease of adapting to the presence of a stranger in our home overnight;

- The generosity of neighbours and staff in our building who have been running errands to pick up prescriptions, food supplies, garbage bags, and other daily living essentials that I run low on, not having left the condo to do any shopping in days. This generosity also extends to the late-night recruitment of a neighbour's strong arms to help me shift Bill back up toward the head of the bed after hours of fidgeting has slipped him so far to the bottom that his feet are getting cramped;

- The emotional roller-coaster ride from last weekend's euphoria after the diagnosis when Bill had his dream of walking with Jesus and felt so at peace about dying, to the day-after-day, increasingly desperate waiting as most of his body shuts down—except for his heart and lungs, trapping the spirit that is ready to fly in a body that is intensely painful;

- My monitoring of his breathing patterns, which fluctuate from quiet and shallow to the distressing prolonged bouts of coughing to the apnoea with its repeated pattern of no intake for twenty-five to thirty seconds followed by a minute or so of regular breathing;

- The myriad of websites that I have surfed studying the indicators of end of life;

- The stress of being convinced that erratic breathing patterns signal that he is about to die within the next few hours;

- The stress of having to psych myself up for another day of watching him in such distress when the erratic breathing patterns do not culminate in death;

- The flood of wonderful e-mail messages that people are sending me, which I read to Bill assuming that he can hear and which give us a tangible sense of being embraced.

I stop for a breath.

Gail studies me for a moment and then says quietly, "You are a bit hyper, aren't you."

She's right.

I let my gaze sweep languorously along the luminous recently restored scenes in each alcove, up the columns to the Baroque frescoes that surrounded the nave, and then back down to the ornate altar heavily adorned with gold plate and weighted with a dozen large silver candlesticks. On the pinnacle of each candlestick a white pillar candle flickered with the light breeze wafting through the doors that opened onto Via Pallazuollo. The strings of the Orchestra Historica di Firenze filled the Vanchetoni Oratory with the music of Scarlatti and Veracini. Bill and I touched hands lightly as the tenor sang *Amarilli* by Caccini and *Every Valley* by Handel, both of which we perform as duets at home with Bill's voice and my piano accompaniment. All the young performers were costumed as early-Renaissance musicians.

This was the essence of tranquillity. A balmy, early autumn evening in Florence. Sitting with my lover enveloped by the art and music of a period we both loved. A time of peace.

Gail has left and there is still an hour or so before Valerie will arrive. I'm sitting beside the bed trying to swab Bill's lips without disturbing him. His eyelids flicker. He is awake. "Hello, my darling. You seem to have had a relatively tranquil day today. I think that you've been asleep most of it." I'm not expecting any response. Conversation is pretty much a thing of the past.

He surprises me with a few soft sounds that are other than his usual breathing noises. He looks directly at me, his eyes not fully open but with his pupils focused, clear, and plaintive. I'm not sure that I can trust my judgment. Is he trying to communicate or am I just projecting my emotional state onto him? He moves his fingers and tightens slightly his grip on my hand. It is not my imagination.

"I know, dear. You want to go. And you're ready to go. And you're at peace about going."

Almost inaudibly, he says, "Yeah."

I take a deep breath and hold his gaze. "I want you to go. We both believe that it will be to a better place, free of the pain you are in now."

"You're right," he says slightly more distinctly.

"I'll be a major mess for a long time, but I'm strong, and we've got lots of friends who will help me. I'll eventually be all right. I want you to know that. You don't have to hang on for my sake."

"Okay," he murmurs and closes his eyes.

"Happy anniversary, my darling. I love you so much," I whisper, tears streaming down my face.

Chapter Twelve—Tuesday, August 18

Dr. Anita Singh, the palliative care doctor, spends an hour and a half with us today. How wonderful to have the doctor come to us and spend so much time assessing, examining, asking questions, prescribing, and listening, listening, listening.

Bill has been formally transferred as a patient from Dr. Hii to Dr. Singh. The paperwork is in order. That means that she can prescribe the medication that she thinks he needs and she will be the person who I call rather than 911 when he dies. Her role is to help me help him die with dignity and the least distress possible. During our wide-ranging conversation, I develop an appreciation for how complex and in some ways how lonely is the role of the palliative care doctor within the medical profession. Many of their peers feel compelled by the Hippocratic Oath, their training, and their personal predispositions to undertake any and all measures that might prolong the patient's life in their care. Palliative care doctors approach their vocation with a radically different orientation, one that many of their colleagues find hard to appreciate. I thank God that we are in the hands of this somewhat marginalised band of angels.

We talk a lot about pain. Since Bill has lost his capacity to speak and hasn't been able to tell me how he is feeling, I have tried to find other ways to assess his level of discomfort. I thought that I had hit on something ingenious when I noticed that his degree of distress could be measured by the intensity with which he furrowed his brow. Turns out my eureka moment is not some Nobel-worthy discovery but a well-established diagnostic tool. Dr. Singh smiles as she realises that she has burst my bubble. Bill hasn't been able to swallow the large Percocet tablets for a couple of days now. I had tried dissolving them in water, but he has had difficulty swallowing that inevitably chalky concoction. Dr. Singh concludes that we have reached the stage where morphine is appropriate. A permanent butterfly port will be installed somewhere around his abdomen to which the morphine pump tube will be connected. She explains that the pump will emit a constant dosage of the pain suppressant, which I will be able to supplement by pushing a button up to three times an hour if he seems to need extra.

We talk about his distress beyond the pain dimension. A week ago, Dr. Hii prescribed Lorazepam, a sedative which might help relax him. Back in those long ago days, Bill was still able to tell me if he felt he needed some and I would give him half or a whole capsule every few hours, which he swallowed with water. Then, as his communication and his swallowing capacity diminished in tandem, I encouraged him to hold it under his tongue until it had dissolved. This is a faster way of getting it into the blood stream than going through the digestive track. He could understand my instructions and could respond in kind. At this point now, he is so frequently asleep or in a seemingly semicomatose state that that option is also limited. I am reluctant to disturb him by manipulating his tongue to get the pill in place. Nor do I want to risk him choking on it if it should get stuck in his throat. Dr. Singh teaches me an ingenious method. You crush the tablet between two small spoons, add a few droplets of water to dissolve it, draw it up in a needleless syringe, and then slowly release the fluid combination into the corner of his mouth. He invariably breathes with his mouth open, as is the case with anyone at this stage, so I have ready access.

I describe those horrible hiccupping-hacking-gagging spells that plague him particularly at night. Not an unheard-of condition, apparently. There is a drug, Buscopan, which can help control that. It will require the insertion of a second butterfly port. Since he is sleeping primarily on his back and not moving a lot around the bed, two butterfly ports may be able to be used, one on each side of his abdomen. I'll then have to insert a syringe into the butterfly port and dispense a dose as he seems to need it. I shudder a bit at the prospect but it doesn't sound too challenging for a squeamish soul like me since I don't have to puncture the skin each time. I'm thankful for those butterfly needles even though I have no idea at this point what they even look like.

Dr. Singh suggests a urinary catheter so we don't have to disturb him as much by changing him. I am not sure which is the lesser of the two evils, but I keep that reservation to myself for the time being.

I assume that Dr. Singh must have a long list of patients and caregivers in similarly stressful circumstances who are anxiously awaiting her arrival, but she gives no hint of rushing through her visit. She asks how I am doing and listens attentively as I describe both the stress of seeing my loved one dying from this horror called pancreatic cancer, and the gratitude I feel for the support of the institutional health care system and the informal network of friends, neighbours, and relatives.

At the door, I clasp her hand with both of mine and shake it firmly, but it still seems a woefully inadequate expression of how appreciative I feel. I return to the living room, sit in my reading chair at the foot of the hospital bed, and let classical music wash over me.

It was the second time we had seen/heard Cecilia Bartoli in concert at Roy Thompson Hall. The first time, we were sitting up with the gods, but on this occasion our seats were in the tenth row of the orchestra. Buying subscription series tickets has definite advantages.

We loved her for her virtuosity, for the repertoire in which she specialised, for the evident fun that she exuded in performing, for not exhibiting the slightest diva stereotypic behaviour on stage and apparently offstage as well, and for her personal dedication to archival research into long-lost masterpieces. Did I mention that she is stunningly beautiful?

After the concert, we decided to do something we almost never did—get an autograph. It had been announced that she would be signing CDs after the performance. We scurried out of the auditorium once we were sure there were no more encores to be heard and yet found a long line already formed in front of the signing table. There was an understandable wait while she recuperated a bit from the concert. But before long, she appeared to another round of applause, seated herself at the table, and started greeting fans and signing their CDs. The RTH staff kept the line moving, ushered everyone along as quickly as possible, and discreetly warned us not to chat with her or take too much time. They evidently did not know with whom they were dealing when it came to Bill. When our turn arrived, I placed our newly purchased copy of her *The Vivaldi Album* on the table and was about to say some platitude that she must have heard a million times already that evening when, without warning, Bill started singing "Amarilli, Mia Bella" by Caccini. Except that he exercised his artistic licence and amended the words to "Cecilia, Mia Bella." Her time-conscious handlers were apoplectic. She waved them off, sat back, and with a huge smile on her face enjoyed being sung to. When he finished, she applauded enthusiastically and complimented him on his fine Italian pronunciation. On the inside cover of our copy of the CD she signed, *Per Guillermo + David con amore (Amarilli) Cecilia Bartoli 20/10/2000.*

Bill's aunt Lenna has a robust spirit. Though not feeling well herself, she insists that her daughter Pat bring her to see Bill. She really wants to have the chance to say good-bye. The only times I had met Lenna were at times of death. She came to Stratford for both the memorial service that we organised for Bill's dad in the spring of 1999 and the celebration of Bill's mom's life that we had in our home in May 2007.

She sits in the chair beside the bed and holds Bill's hand. We have no way of knowing if Bill is conscious of her presence, but that doesn't inhibit Lenna. She chatters to Bill about days gone by and the many times that she had to scold him for constantly getting into mischief.

Within a month, Lenna is diagnosed with cancer.

A little while after Pat and Lenna leave, there is a gentle knock on the door. Richard, a former colleague of mine at the United Church as well as a good friend, is standing at the door proffering two dishes of delicious casseroles from Cumbrae's on Church Street.

Quintessentially considerate, he says, "I don't want to disturb you and Bill. I won't come in. I just wanted to deliver these because I was afraid that you might not be eating properly." I take the bag and haul him inside. I have an agenda.

After giving him some quiet time at Bill's bedside, I ask, "Would you pray with us please, Richard?" Without hesitation, we grasp hands including Bill's and Richard prays.

Richard was one of the main organisers of the two retirement parties that the United Church put on for me and acted as the emcee at both—an afternoon tea in December 2006 mainly for staff of the United Church's General Council Office in which I had worked for thirty-one years and an evening dinner in January 2007 to which many colleagues from both within and beyond the United Church were invited. Both events included speeches, some of the roasting variety.

At the January dinner, I was honoured with tributes by various persons who had been colleagues over the years, including retired Senator Rev. Dr. Lois Wilson, who served for a decade on a federal environmental commission studying options for nuclear waste from Canadian reactors; the Hon. Rev. David MacDonald, who as an MP had chaired Canada's first parliamentary environment committee for a long time from the late 1980s onwards; and Elizabeth May, who I had met first when she was the executive director of the Sierra Club and who now was the leader of the Green Party of Canada. After they and numerous other speakers, including my brother Rick, had had their say, it was Bill's turn. He stood for a moment at the microphone, looked at me, and said dryly, "So, I guess you're not just a pretty face after all." It brought the house down.

I spend the evening getting more of the memorial service prepared. A friend and professional musician, David Ambrose, has agreed to participate and may recruit some of his colleagues to do a group number. He's Denny's partner. Boris Trevius, the organist at our church, will play. The three ministers associated with Saint Luke's United Church, Hoon Kim, Gordon Winch, and Malcolm Finlay, have all been in touch regularly over the past days giving us much-needed pastoral support. They will take part in the service. I knew that I didn't want any grand eulogy. Bill would hate that. I thought that it would be fun to have a number of people provide brief reflections on the Bill they knew and loved. Those who I've contacted have all expressed how honoured they feel to be asked. I'm deeply touched and a little overwhelmed. So far I've gotten positive responses from Doug O'Neill, Huda Abbasi, Laurice Mahli, Peter Spencer and Eric Marshall (doing their bit as the lovable couple they are), Tamara Glazier, and Denny Young. One of the things that I like is that they represent quite different connections with Bill and me over our life.

I plan to write some sort of theological reflection of my own for the service, but I am 99 percent sure that I will not have the stamina to speak the words myself. So I've asked Rob Oliphant and he has agreed to read it for me and add his own comments. Marco Fiola, his partner, is going to read a piece about Bill's love of languages. Whenever we had children in our home, especially sitting on the veranda in Stratford, Bill used to love reading limericks with them from his old copy of *The Complete Nonsense of Edward Lear*. Our Stratford neighbours, Maureen Argon and Brendan Howley, whose children have been among those kids, will read some selections from the book.

I've figured out a way to get extra music into the service. I'm sorting though our CD collection selecting a variety of classical and popular pieces that are either meaningful to Bill and me, reflect important sentiments, or are performed by artists who we love and may have seen in concert. David Ambrose has agreed to help me get them burned onto a disk. I'll have it playing before and after the service and as background during the funeral home visitation on the Saturday. Bill might find some of my selections verging on the maudlin, but this is my party and I'll cry if I want to.

I'm pleased with how it is coming together. When I step back and reflect on what it is that I'm actually organising, I'm not pleased.

Chapter Thirteen—Wednesday, August 19

Meynardo has a day off. Zaid, his replacement as homecare nurse for our neighbourhood, arrives on schedule. I introduce him to Bill, but Bill makes no response. His loss of language and virtually all other communication capacity is painful for me. It must be tearing him apart inside.

After checking Bill's vital signs, he inserts the first of the butterfly ports and hooks up the morphine. The morphine pump is a compact little machine that hangs suspended on the rail of Bill's hospital bed and into which Zaid mounts one of the cartridges delivered by the pharmacy late yesterday. Now, our refrigerator holds not only milk, chicken, and broccoli, but cartridges of a "highly potent, opiate, analgesic, psychoactive drug" (according to Wikipedia). He explains the pump dials to me; specifically the dosage one that I can press up to three times an hour if I judge that Bill is in distress and needs more than the preset drip.

There is a piece missing from the second butterfly port delivered by the pharmacy, so Zaid is not able to install it. The Buscopan drug has arrived, which is supposed to help suppress Bill's awful hiccup-coughing spells, and I'm anxious that he have access to it as soon as possible. Without a useable butterfly port, the other option is that

I administer it directly by syringe at the recommended frequency. I'm not a big needle kind of guy, so I feel uneasy about this scenario. But given the alternative, this is an inhibition worth surmounting. Zaid gives me a tutorial on sterilizing the site, grasping a bit of skin between my thumb and forefinger, and inserting the needle. I do it initially under Zaid's watchful eye. Bill doesn't flinch, so I guess my skill is passable.

The pharmacy also neglected to send the sterilized water that is necessary to inflate the balloon for the catheter. The option of a catheter had come up yesterday with Dr. Singh because using one would reduce the amount that we had to move Bill and hence lessen the pain caused when we change him. However, thinking now more about what is involved with the attachment of a catheter, I am not as enthusiastic. Most of his internal organs seemed to be shutting down in any case, so there is not as much changing that we have to do on a daily basis. I'm starting to think that the status quo is the lesser of the two evils.

Bill loved learning languages. Partly, it was the musician in him, the beauty of hearing the words spoken or sung.

Spanish had a big place in his heart. He spoke Spanish to any Hispanic he met on the street. He jabbered away to a Mexican friend in Stratford. He had long, gossipy conversations with the housekeeper at the guest house in Puerto Vallarta where we spent every February. He enjoyed conversations with the Spanish-speaking staff at Verve, the new condominium building we moved into in October 2008.

About ten years ago, after regaling his mother with endless stories of how much at home he felt when we were travelling in Mexico and how easily the language seemed to come to him, she looked him in the eye and said, "I guess it is about time I told you something."

"What?"

She hesitated. "Your grandfather is not who you think he is."

"What?"

"Hardly anyone in the family knows about this. I've never told you or anyone else about this except your dad, of course. Frankly, I've always been pretty embarrassed about it." Long pause. "You know that my mother, your grandmother, was not all that keen on family life." Bill had heard lots of stories over the years about the two marriages, about how she would dump off her kids at relatives' homes when she tired of them, a little bit about her life in vaudeville. "Well, she had an affair and bore two children out of wedlock. I was one of them."

"Oh my God. Are you serious?"

"This is not something I would joke about," she said sternly.

"Sorry. Sure. Please go on."

"My father, your grandfather, your real grandfather, was Mexican." Bill sat dumbstruck. After a moment, she asked, "Are you upset?" He just stared at her incredulous. Bill at a loss for words. Imagine. Adelle ventured on, "I guess my mother met him through the show business. He was a trick rider with a travelling Mexican rodeo. Apparently, his stage name was Mexican Joe."

Bill exploded in laughter, jumped up, kissed his mother, and started dancing around the room. "This is fantastic. Absolutely incredible. I'm part Mexican. That explains so much. Do you know anything more about him?"

"Only his name and what I've told you."

"I'm thrilled, Mom."

"And I'm relieved, I guess. Now we don't have to talk about it anymore."

Bill's most recent project was to teach himself Italian. He loved travelling in Italy. He loved the operas of Verdi and Puccini. He loved the films of Fellini and Visconti. He loved Italian design. He decided that he just had to speak and understand the language fluently. He took night school courses and had workbooks from which he taught himself the grammar and vocabulary. For Bill, the culmination of learning Italian was going to be to be able to read Dante's *The Divine Comedy* in the original. He wanted to go to Italy soon and spend a year studying Italian and art. He didn't make it.

Tamara, a former neighbour from Stratford with whom we have kept in close contact since she moved to Toronto, comes by late in the afternoon bearing dinner supplies. It is tough for her to see Bill like this. He has been a great support for her during her transition leaving her Stratford life. She will miss him. She is determined to support us during this difficult transition in our lives. And she does so practically for me with this food and emotionally for me through her regular phone calls and e-mail messages. I take advantage of her visit to distract myself a bit from what is going within the walls of our condo and remind myself that there is life still going on outside. I ask her about her preparations for the start of the new school year. She has a great job as a consultant with a large school board north of the city.

Bill was a born teacher. He loved helping children learn.

He believed in their original goodness.

He was strict with children whether working with them individually or in a group, but it was a discipline grounded in his respect for them.

Children adored him.

Bill had infinite patience with children.

With adults, not as much.

It's reassuring to hear the soft buzz of the morphine pump as it automatically dispenses the magic potion several times an hour. I have not been hesitant to manually add my contribution. The pump electronics are programmed not to allow more than three extra dosages an hour, so I don't run the risk of giving him an overdose. The morphine, combined with the dissolved sedative that I slip into his open mouth periodically, seems to be limiting his distress at least according to my scientific furrowed-brow measuring stick. His breathing is even and quiet this evening, his eyes closed. I presume he is sleeping. I'm hoping that he is at rest. *Will tonight be the night that he slips into permanent rest?*

Joy has replaced Valerie as the overnight nurse for the next few days. The two of them are both from the islands. Their comforting presence in our home during the night hours makes me feel like a down-filled blanket has been wrapped around our trembling lives. Joy and I change Bill and gently apply the skin cream. It is helping. There is less chapping and redness today. Joy is a knitter. I say good-night as she settles into the big reading chair at the foot of Bill's bed and launches into her silent sweater-making.

In the library, I read the most recent e-mails of support. I then compose and send out my fifth update:

Dear family and friends,

Heartfelt thanks for the wonderful support that you have been providing to Bill and me—practical, emotional, and spiritual. A number of you have confirmed from people who you know experiencing the same thing that we are currently experiencing—that is, pancreatic cancer is indeed one of the most difficult to detect and once diagnosed one of the fastest to metastasize into other organs, making it largely inoperable and untreatable. The pace of Bill's physical deterioration since his August 7 diagnosis is truly mind-numbing.

The major development recently is that as of today we have progressed to the morphine pump stage. That became quite important since he has not been able to swallow the pain medication pills for about three days. Though he is virtually unable to speak and tell us how he is feeling, there were enough body signs to indicate that he was in considerable pain and distress. The pump provides a consistent low dosage of morphine that I can supplement up to three times an hour if it is apparent that he is in discomfort.

The morphine was authorised by the palliative care doctor who spent almost an hour and a half here yesterday doing a thorough exam of Bill, interviewing me about his medical history, assessing our home care situation, and authorising several further additions to the care package. I am so appreciative and still in awe of the amount and quality of in-home care (material and personnel) that we are receiving, allowing us thus to keep Bill at home until the end.

From small gestures and his occasional very soft whispering, I believe that he is still hearing and comprehending most of what I say to him. A recent example:

David: I know that you are ready and wanting to go.

Bill: Yeah.

David: And I want you to go. We both believe that it will be to a better place free of the pain you are in now.

Bill: You're right.

David: I'll be a mess, but I'm strong. We've got lots of friends who will support me. I will eventually be all right. You don't have to hang on for my sake.

Bill: Okay.

Because he still has hearing, I have soft music playing constantly in our condo. Usually, it is classical chamber or Baroque, but sometimes a vocal artist for whom Bill feels a particular affection (e.g., Cecilia Bartoli, Keely Smith, Blossom Dearie, Dinah Washington, Kiri te Kanawa, among others).

Though the palliative care doctor couldn't/wouldn't give me a very specific projection of how long he has left, she confirmed my anticipation that we are likely talking a week at most. Bill might surprise us, though—that heart of his, which worried him during his life because of an inherent weakness, now seems to be mimicking the Energizer bunny.

Based on the assumption that he will die in the next week or so, my current planning in terms of timing of funeral arrangements is to hold them on the weekend of September 12–13. On Saturday, September 12, there would be an opportunity for visitation at Rosar-Morrison Funeral Home, 467 Sherbourne Street (just south of Wellesley) from 2:00 to 4:00 p.m. and 7:00 to 9:00 p.m. The memorial service would be held on Sunday, September 13 at 2:00 p.m. at Saint Luke's United Church, 353 Sherbourne Street (at Carlton). I'm pleased that a number of friends of Bill and mine who are in the arts will participate in the service.

Love to you all, David

Chapter Fourteen—Thursday, August 20

Meynardo is back today. His examination of Bill confirms that he does not seem to be in distress. We talk about the catheter question. I can tell that he has some hesitation about utilising it. I learn that it is a more complicated process than I had first imagined. Its intrusiveness, figuratively and literally, becomes starkly apparent to me. I decide that that is a road we will not go down. We'll leave Bill as undisturbed as possible.

The supplies for the second butterfly port have arrived, so Meynardo is able to install it. I still have to insert the Buscopan-filled syringes into the port every few hours and that operation is a bit tricky because of the spring valve in the port. I have to press the syringe head down into it until it catches, turn the syringe so it locks, and then empty the contents into the port. I worry that the pressure that I have to apply might hurt Bill if there is any irritation that the permanent butterfly is causing under his skin. But there is no redness around either port, which suggests that they remain clean and uninfected. Bill hasn't been making any sound when I give him a dose of the Buscopan, so I figure I'm doing it okay. It is certainly better than having to break the skin each time with a needle-tipped syringe like I was doing yesterday.

Thank goodness for small mercies.

On Tuesday, August 4, we headed out to Mississauga to attend a memorial service for the mother of a friend. We had first met Doug over twenty years ago when we were all living in the Beach area of Toronto. Doug was one of the Toronto gay community's most ardent volunteers. Bill and I used to marvel at his organising skill in community events and his patience when confronted with the ineptitude and bickering inherent in many voluntary organisations. We hadn't seen a lot of Doug over recent years after he moved out west for work.

When we arrived in the lobby of the funeral home, I could see the startled expression in Doug's eyes, present for a moment but then quickly suppressed, at the sight of Bill in the wheelchair. Bill spoke to Doug about the likely peaceful nature of his mother's death, words that Doug found deeply reassuring. In a later conversation, Doug told me that though Bill's physical gauntness was a shock to see, he was nevertheless encouraged at his clear-eyed and tranquil demeanour.

Doug delivered the eulogy at his mother's service with wit and grace. Little did any of us realise how soon death and another memorial service would intrude on our lives.

I notice in my calendar that we are supposed to have an appointment at Toronto East General Hospital this afternoon at 2:00 p.m. for a pulmonary test. I am hoping that one branch of the hospital talks to another. The pulmonary test had been set up after Bill saw a specialist at TEGH in mid-July. That was at the time when the only trouble showing up on tests was the spasming oesophagus. The specialist had prescribed medication to heal the oesophagus, which was supposed to produce results within a month, hence the August 20 pulmonary test. A CAT scan and a pancreatic cancer diagnosis on August 7 at TEGH have somehow insinuated themselves into that original game plan.

I phone the hospital and get through to the appropriate department. No, they had not heard that Bill would not be able to make his appointment today. I look over at my semiconscious lover in the living room hospital bed and try to imagine him with a mask on his face, electrodes attached to his chest, while running on a treadmill. The nurse on the line expresses her deepest sympathy when I explain our situation. This is no automaton on the other end of the line just readjusting the day's appointment schedule. Again, I am impressed and appreciative of the humanity that we are encountering at every level of the health care system as we live through this nightmare. Perhaps the system is not as efficient as it might be. But what they lack in interdepartmental communication, they more than make up for in supportive caregiving.

I've been too busy this morning to have my first cup of coffee. I pour it now, step out onto the balcony, and sink into the lounge chair, looking down Wellesley Street into our gaybourhood.

I don't remember who called us. A phone tree or rather a forest of phone trees had materialised around the city alerting people that there had been another series of police raids at gay bathhouses in Toronto and that a demonstration was planned for this evening, June 20, 1981, starting at the intersection of Yonge and Wellesley.

Bathhouses were not our scene, but Bill and I shared with many other gays a visceral revulsion at the police harassment of these gay social establishments over the previous months. What was the great threat to society presented by what these consenting adults did behind closed doors in private facilities where no one was being hurt? With the addition of those arrested in the raids a few days earlier, over 330 gay men were now facing charges. Bathhouses were often frequented by men living in the closet in their personal or professional lives. News of their arrests could lead to being fired, evicted, family breakdown, and suicide. But beyond the specifics of the charges, the bathhouse raids had come to symbolise a particular public manifestation of the day-to-day persecution that many gays experienced in their own lives. Demonstrations to protest the bathhouse raids became a collective outlet in our struggle for gay human rights and protection from discrimination.

Bill found a couple sheets of newsprint in our apartment and we hastily prepared signs. On our way down on the elevator, we were joined by a few friends heading to the protest. Though we had ready access to the subway from our building near Danforth and Victoria Park, we decided to take the car. There had been an increase in gay-bashing around the city by young straight guys seemingly emboldened by the police assaults on the gay community. We thought that with our signs we would be safer in our private vehicle than in a public subway car.

By the time we got to Yonge and Wellesley around 10:30 p.m., there were already hundreds of people crowding the sidewalk and spilling over onto the street. The demonstration was planned to proceed up Yonge Street to Bloor Street and then east two blocks and end in front of Toronto Police Headquarters on Jarvis Street. Just a little after 11:00 p.m., over two thousand of us took over the main street in Toronto and started to proceed north. Bill and I were near the front. We soon saw a phalanx of riot police linked arm-in-arm stretching across Yonge Street at the intersection of St. Joseph, one block north of Wellesley. The marchers moved closer. The police tightened ranks. Someone yelled, "Sit down. Sit down." Immediately, we all sat on the street, thousands of gay men occupying one of the city's main thoroughfares, nervous about the baton-wielding police twenty feet in front of us, but bolstered by our outrage at the institutional persecution that we were experiencing as a community.

The intense standoff, or rather sit-down, showed no sign of resolution until we noticed a couple of the demonstration organisers cautiously approaching the police. For about five or ten minutes, negotiations proceeded while a series of chants erupted through the crowd. Some resolution was reached. The order was given and the police moved off the street and lined up along the sidewalk. The crowd cheered. We stood up and resumed the march north. At the intersection of Yonge and Bloor the crowd staged another sit-down, this time not as passive resistance against hundreds of police blocking our path but rather as a spontaneous demonstration that this was our city too and we would no longer settle for being treated as second class.

We milled around with some of our friends for a while after the speeches that concluded the demonstration, and then headed home. After we left the downtown, a series of incidents occurred with queer-bashers brandishing pieces of lumber and attacking people in the dispersing crowd. Gays who tried to protect those who were being attacked were in turn pursued by police. A number of gay men ended up with injuries requiring treatment in the emergency department of nearby Wellesley Hospital. Six people were charged with assault and obstructing justice, none of them being those who attacked the gay demonstrators.

Sandra, the supervisor from Community Care Access Centre who has Bill as one of her clients, comes by for a visit. She apologises for not having been here sooner. She says that she likes to get to know clients under her care early in the process. Though this is the first time that I have met her, Bill and I have been experiencing her coordination efforts for almost two weeks. It is CCAC that contracts with Saint Elizabeth Health Care, which has assigned the nurse Meynardo to visit us daily, and it is through CCAC that we have personal support workers (PSWs) coming for two hours daily from

Toronto Homemakers Services to help me care for Bill and to sit with him overnight while I get some rest.

I express my deep appreciation to Sandra, but she modestly brushes it off. "That is what we are here for. I'm pleased that the services are working out well for you. I'm just so sorry for Bill's serious situation and what the two of you are going through."

I get us each a cup of tea.

"One of our biggest challenges," she continues, "is letting people know that these services are available for caring for loved ones in their own homes. Most people assume that when you get as ill as Bill, there is no option but to be hospitalised."

"I am so grateful that we have been able to keep him at home. This is obviously the last home that we will have as a couple and it means so much to us that we can spend his last days together here. He designed much of this condo and loves it. It's much, much quieter than a hospital room would be, which reduces the stress on him. I can control the environment. As you can tell, music is obviously very important in our lives. I can have soft classical music playing here all the time. I'm sure he hears it. I can also have much more of a role caring for him than if I had to relinquish that responsibility to professionals in a hospital setting. I could go on and on."

"I hope you do. We need ambassadors like you to get the word out to others who could benefit."

Bill and I have had nine homes over the course of our thirty-three years together.

We started in my apartment at 100 Wellesley Street East, a building that we can see from the balcony of our current home at Verve. The first condo that we bought and moved into in 1977 was in Massey Square at Danforth and Victoria Park. After a few years there, we also bought a cottage up in the Kawartha Lakes District that we had for about five years. We sold the Massey Square condo in

1984 and moved to a tiny but historically interesting little house on Kenilworth Street in the Beach. Many years ago, it apparently had served as the local post office. In 1986, we moved over a couple of blocks to Lee Avenue and stayed there for about twelve years. It was while on Lee that we operated a bed-and-breakfast business from our house. In 1991, we bought the Stratford house and for a while had the two properties. That got to be too much work, so we sold the Lee Avenue house and bought a bachelor condo on Woodbine Avenue between Queen Street and the lake. We sold that in 2005 and moved downtown to a one-bedroom condo in the new development RadioCity, which was built in conjunction with the National Ballet School facilities. While we were in Puerto Vallarta in 2006, we came to the conclusion that retiring in Stratford was not the best plan anymore, mainly because our primary health care providers on whom we would depend as we aged were based in Toronto. But the RadioCity condo would not be big enough for us to live in full-time. We had tons of books, the piano, art, and furniture in the Stratford house that we would want to keep. So we started looking around at options for a larger condo downtown and that's when we stumbled into the Tridel store on Carlton, met Teresa, fell in love with the Verve project, and bought our condo preconstruction in March 2006. We moved into it in October 2008.

In each of these nine residences, Bill had the good taste, design skill, and enthusiasm to make them into beautiful living environments.

Nine seems like a lot of residences to live in over that amount of time. It is. But each move was well thought out from the perspective of our quality of life and its financial soundness. I can't take much credit for that. Bill was the one with the vision. Left to my own devices and if Bill and I hadn't met, I would probably still be living in my apartment at 100 Wellesley Street East.

Before I knew him, in addition to teaching, Bill had bought numerous houses, fixed them up, and sold them. He also had built and sold several cottages. When we first met in 1976, Bill had a house in Lawrence Park. At some point early on, he must have sold it.

It seems strange to me on reflection, but we never talked in our early days about our respective financial situations with the exception of one conversation shortly after we met when he wanted to know if I still had any student loans (I didn't) or car loans (I did). When we bought our first home together in January 1977, the condo at Massey Square, we both contributed fifty-fifty to the down payment. From then on and throughout our thirty-three years, we shared the living costs equitably.

I have no idea what Bill's financial resources were when we started living together. I suspect that they were considerable.

I remember that he seemed concerned that we enter into our new relationship on as equitable a footing as possible.

At some point in the first few years, I came across an appreciation card addressed to him from Mother Teresa's foundation. I asked him about it. He replied cryptically that he had given all his money to her after we met. I didn't press him for more details and he didn't offer any.

Chapter Fifteen—Friday, August 21

Meynardo comes twice today.

His regular morning examination yields continuing stable results in blood pressure and pulse. I'm disappointed as I expect Bill would be, were he aware. Both Bill and I are waiting for his heart to manifest empirical signs of its preparation to cease and desist.

His liver function does seem to have pretty much come to a halt. I do not have to change him anymore.

This can't go on much longer.

God, why don't you let him go?

For days I have been surfing the net for articles on the signs of end of life. The ones I find are pretty consistent with one another. A hospice website gives me the most tangible descriptors. Some indicators apply to Bill. We're well past others that are listed. A few have not yet surfaced.

Changes in breathing patterns are what I notice the most. But I don't know what they mean. Sometimes, his breathing is very quiet and shallow, hardly detectable. He has occasional apnoea where his breathing stops altogether for extended periods of time. But then there will be a dramatic episode that lasts a long time where he appears to be gasping for breath. It is during those episodes that I am most convinced that the end is near. But then he returns to the quiet pattern and my death watch is forced into retreat again.

One thing I notice is that Bill has not moved at all since last night. His head, his legs, his arms, even his fingers are in exactly the same position. Meynardo recommends that I turn him from side to side every few hours. He shows me how to prop a pillow under his back to keep him stabilised on one side and then the other. I hear his advice but am hesitant to disturb Bill if I move him around like that.

Meynardo's second visit a few hours later is in order to adjust the morphine pump after he receives instructions from Dr. Singh to increase the hourly dosage.

I sit and wait.

I pace and wait.

I read e-mails and wait.

I get the *Globe and Mail* delivered to my door every day. I have the time but somehow not the energy to read it. I haven't for a week. *Is the world still going on outside?*

Two weeks ago, on what I have come to call the diagnosis weekend when Bill and I had such wonderful reminiscent and gratitude-filled discussions, one of the subjects was what he would like for his memorial service. He wanted music to be a big component.

He said, "It would be wonderful if Ashley would come and play. I'd like that."

Ashley MacIsaac, a well-known fiddler originally from Cape Breton, lived in the RadioCity development at the same time as we did from 2006 to 2008. He and Bill became friends. They had a similar kind of mischievous spirit and they would have animated, irreverent conversations when they'd meet. I had been trying to get in touch with him in recent days. It took a while for my e-mails to work their way through his website to him personally. I've now gotten a response. He's very sad to hear about Bill. He'll do his best to arrange his schedule so that he can be in Toronto the day of his memorial. He writes, "I will do my best to bring a little music to a service when we honour Bill."

I sit in the chair beside the bed and hold Bill's hand. "Bill, darling, I don't know if you can hear me or if you are awake. It looks like you'll get your wish. Ashley will play at your memorial service."

Bill and I have been long-term members of the Art Gallery of Ontario and the Royal Ontario Museum.

The last time that we visited the AGO together was on June 3. We went to see an exhibit on Surrealism with our friends and Verve neighbours Frank and Armand. Bill and I got there early, so we spent some time wandering around other parts of the gallery and having a coffee in the members' lounge. In a room filled with paintings by Kurelek, we ran into a dear longtime friend who lives just a block away from us. Doug is in the publishing business and had squeezed some time out of his day to come and soak his spirit in the ambiance of the AGO. We were all in a quiet contemplative mood. It was a nice encounter.

Bill's and my last visit to the ROM together was on June 29, the day after the Toronto Gay Pride weekend. We had tickets for the *Dead Sea Scrolls* exhibition. Bill, in the wheelchair, had some difficulty reading the descriptions in the various display cabinets. I think a bigger problem was that he just didn't have much energy. After a while, he told me to leave him by the side and wander around on my own until I had seen everything that I wanted. When I was finished and went to retrieve him, he struck me as such a lonely figure dozing quietly in his chair by the side wall.

Doug comes for a visit this evening. We had all had a lot of fun together at parties years ago when we were much younger. Bill used to tease Doug about a particularly amorous time in Denny's kitchen on one such occasion. Our paths didn't cross for a number of years and so it has been good to reconnect with Doug recently, at the AGO in June and at our Pride party.

Doug and I talk quietly next to Bill's bed and reminisce about the past.

Doug had brought a lovely poem that he thought Bill might like. He sits by the bed and softly reads it to him.

Flora is the night nurse who arrives at 11:00 p.m. She is filling in for Joy who has a family commitment. I explain that there is little to do, given Bill's state. We chat for a bit and then I head to bed.

I have just laid down when I hear Bill breathing in a very laboured manner. This sounds different than the other variations. I jump out of bed and come back to sit by him. This strikes me as serious. I silently chastise myself. *How can it get more serious than it already has been?* But that's my feeling. This may be the last stage. We may be very close.

For the first time, I am uncomfortable with the presence of a support person. I have nothing against Flora. It is rather that I really want to be alone with Bill if he is about to die. I don't want to have to be concerned with the presence of another person, a stranger, in our midst. Awkwardly, I explain how I am feeling and ask her if she would mind leaving. She is a little taken aback and worried that she has done something that has displeased me. I assure her that that is not the case and that I will ensure that she gets paid for the night's shift. I just really want to be alone with Bill. She leaves graciously.

Bill and I are alone as we approach the end.

This room feels like sacred space. We are alone and yet not alone. I implore God to let his spirit be released from his body. I make a pot of coffee and settle into the big armchair at the foot of his bed.

Chapter Sixteen—Saturday, August 22

Bill is still here.

He had major breathing episodes for most of the night. That's not a very technical way of describing them. He was straining hard and there were loud, raspy, guttural sounds as he inhaled and exhaled.

I phone the Toronto Homemaker Service number. It is Saturday morning so I guess there is no one in the office. I leave a voicemail message asking them to cancel Nelson's visit today. Nelson is the PSW who came last weekend and is scheduled to attend to Bill this weekend as well. My judgment, though, is that Bill doesn't need bathing anymore and the less he is disturbed, the better.

I also ask that they not send anyone for the overnight period. I don't think that Bill will be alive by tonight. But even if he is, I will want to be alone with him.

I hope I am making the right decision.

It was a busy Gay Pride celebration the last weekend in June. Bill was tired during much of the month and in quite a bit of discomfort. Under normal circumstances, I would have suggested that we should cancel our Pride party this year. I am sure he would have agreed without hesitation. But I don't even raise the possibility. I want to go ahead with it. I have the unsettling suspicion that it might be Bill's last. I want our friends to be able to see him one more time in a festive context. I know that I am pushing, but I think it is worth it. I think that he and they will appreciate it if my premonitions bear out.

We usually had our Pride weekend open house party on the Saturday afternoon. That way it didn't interfere with our attending the big parade on Sunday. It also meant that I could go out to one of the big dances on Saturday night without worrying that I had to avoid a hangover and be in good enough shape to host legions of party boys the next day.

We usually had a theme with corresponding food. One of the years that we were in the condo at RadioCity, Bill made twenty quiches. Not so subtly, the parody was of course "real men don't eat quiche." Our unit at RadioCity was a small one-bedroom. I think the official size was 557 square feet. That worked well enough for the two of us on our nights in the city. At that time, we were spending a lot of time at the Stratford house. But it was a bit cosy when you have thirty gay men over for brunch. We were on the twenty-fifth floor and our balcony looked down on the sound stage at the corner of Church Street and Wood Street, so at least half of the guests could crowd out onto the balcony, eat, drink, and listen to the entertainment down below. Another year, at RadioCity, we went Mexican. One of our neighbours owned a small Mexican restaurant a few blocks away and we had him cater it. We provided the *cerveza*.

This being our first Pride weekend in the new Verve condo, I was anxious to show it off to as many of our gay friends as possible. Plus, I really wanted them to have a chance to see Bill once more. So I invited lots of people. I distributed invitations to gay friends in the building and sent e-mail versions far and wide including to some of our PV friends who I knew wouldn't be able to make it but who would enjoy being invited anyway. The invitations read "PANSY PRIDE PIZZA PARTY—You are invited to Bill and David's Toronto Pride Open House for Gay Boys, Saturday June 27, 2009, 12 noon to 3:00 p.m., suite 3109 at The Verve," and were adorned with a gay flag and a picture of a cluster of pansies, which Bill always referred to as "our national flower." We had around fifty people show up. Again, it was a sunny day so many of them congregated on the balcony, which in this apartment looks directly down Wellesley Street toward the hub of Pride activity at Church and Wellesley. Disco music bounced off the walls. We hired a cute young man to keep everyone supplied with drinks and the table replete with fresh warm pizza, which I had arranged to be delivered in batches on a regular basis during the course of the party.

Bill sat regally in the big armchair in the living room receiving obeisance from his friends and admirers, joking, admonishing, and generally maintaining his reputation as the life of the party. Almost invariably, though, most of our guests came to me at some point before they left and asked the same question, "Is Bill okay? He doesn't look well." The detail of my response depended on whether they were close friends or just acquaintances. At that point, at the end of June, all of us were still over a month away from knowing the real answer to the question.

On the Sunday morning, we went to a much more lavish catered brunch at a nearby house. Richard was a real estate agent who we had used on some of our sales/purchases over the years, but more importantly he was a very good friend. His house is only a block from our condo, so we walked. Bill resisted taking the wheelchair. He used a cane and leaned heavily on my arm. We encountered several friends on our way to Richard's and on the way home. They were shocked at how slowly and feebly Bill was walking. At the brunch, Bill sat in the living room while I ate my way through the delicious buffet and brought him a small plate of samples, only a few of which he touched. Dear Richard remained the gregarious host and was so hospitable but was clearly concerned about Bill.

Our friend Doug, who also lives nearby, had invited us for a late Sunday afternoon party, but Bill was too exhausted. I was delighted and relieved that he had been able to make it through our Saturday party and Richard's Sunday brunch and to see so many of our friends. My mission was accomplished.

Nelson is at the door. Evidently the weekend voicemail system doesn't work so well. He did not get the message that I was cancelling his visit. When I tell him that we don't need him, he looks crestfallen. His expression doesn't change when I assure him that I'll call the agency on Monday and make sure he gets paid for the visit even though we are not using him. I realise that his disappointment is not out of concern for his pay. He was looking forward to helping us. Under normal circumstances, I would invite him in. But these are not normal circumstances.

Dianne, the nursing supervisor for Saint Elizabeth Health Care, is filling in for Meynardo today. She can see that there is not a lot more any of us can do for Bill. She spends her time talking to me about how I am doing. Her focus is on how to support me, the caregiver. She is concerned that I asked Flora to leave last night and that I have cancelled the night nurse for tonight. I know that she has my best interests at heart. But I remain firm. I am sure we are in the very last stages and I want to be alone with him.

The weekend after our Pansy Pride Pizza Party, Bill came along with me to Stratford for his one and only trip to the house this summer. We were getting ready for selling the Stratford house. It would be a private deal since we had been approached by several couples interested in buying it when we were ready to sell. With his usual propensity to be well organised, Bill was anxious to get rid of as much of our stuff from the house as possible and to make a buck in the process. So we put an ad in the local paper for a yard sale on Saturday, July 4.

I had another agenda. I e-mailed most of our good friends in Stratford.

A short note to let you know that Bill and I expect to be in Stratford for a few days this coming weekend (July 3–5). As most of you know, Bill's health has not been good for the past several months and this will be his first trip to Stratford since last Christmas. How frequently we will be able to come up during the summer will depend on his stamina. Our new condo here in Toronto is very comfortable for him and is closer to his health providers so he feels more secure in Toronto. We are planning to have a garage sale on Saturday morning from 9:00 a.m. to about 12 noon. If you're in the vicinity of 75 Nile and want to drop by for a cup of coffee, we'd be happy to see you.

This was for our Stratford friends the equivalent of the Pride party invitation for our Toronto gay friends. I didn't know how many more times they would have a chance to see Bill.

Fortunately, I had not been too subtle. Many of our friends dropped around on Saturday morning. Bill didn't have the strength to be moving around as he used to during garage sales, but his salesmanship spirit was undiminished. From his perch on the front lawn, sitting in as comfortable a chair as I could find for him, he kept up a steady banter with both friends and strangers, selling a raft of things, and making almost five hundred dollars in the process. Friends spoke to me discreetly or e-mailed me later expressing their shock at how frail he was. But in their intercourse with him that day, everything was levity and profitability.

It was the last time that any of them saw him alive.

I am really perplexed at Bill's motionlessness. He hasn't moved since yesterday morning. Even the way the fingers of his right hand are poised against his face has not shifted in the least.

He is not sleeping all of the time. His head is resting with the left cheek against the pillow. The left eye is closed all the time but the right eye is partially open from time to time. I can see the pupil of his eye and it looks like he is looking at me. I take that as an indication that he is awake and cognizant so I keep up a soft but steady conversation.

I reassure him that I am here.

I say that I love him.

I tell him that it is okay that he goes if he is ready. That is probably the stupidest thing that I have ever said in my life.

Later in the afternoon, my cousin Joan comes down from Newmarket to spend a few hours with us. She is a retired nurse, so she has history with seeing people in the dying process. But this is family, plus it brings back vivid memories for her of being with her dad, my uncle Norm, as he died of cancer many years ago.

I draw a lot of support from her. Not only can I talk about all the medical stuff, which helps me exorcise some of the pent-up stress about Bill's suffering, but we can reminisce about family experiences that we had together as kids. I convince her to stay for supper so she can help me eat some of the food that friends and neighbours have so generously brought me.

Before Simon there was Sebastian and before Sebastian there was Rufus. They were all orange tabbies. We named Rufus after a friend of ours who had a great head of blond hair. Rufus, *Homo sapiens*, was not amused.

We had Rufus when we had the cottage. One winter, we were amazed at how he would lie right under the wood stove. His fur would get very warm. We didn't know how he could stand it. Turns out it was therapeutic. He was dying of feline leukaemia. The heat apparently dulled the pain. I guess we weren't very bright not to have picked up the signs.

I wonder if I'm any brighter now.

When we had Sebastian, we also had Barcey. Barcey was a big beige-and-white rabbit. We bought him from the humane society the week after we had returned from a trip to Barcelona. Hence, Barcelona Bunny. Barcey for short. Barcey loved to run after Sebastian and nudge him until Sebastian would start grooming Barcey. But Sebastian was much older than Barcey and didn't have the stamina or the patience or sufficient maternal instinct to take responsibility for a toddler. He would saunter away. Barcey would hop after him and the routine would start again until Sebastian would finally crawl into a hiding place where Barcey couldn't find him. Barcey was cute but a slow learner.

Bill and I are alone now for the night. It was a beautiful sunset. I wish he could have seen it.

Back at the computer, I play and replay and replay a collage of photographs that I have put together courtesy of Bill Gates or whatever minion of his designed the program Photo Story for Windows. It starts with an antique (sorry, darling) picture of Bill at two months in a baby carriage and then one as a handsome teenager. From there, we move into a retrospective of our thirty-three years together:

- Bill and David in the Massey Square condo
- Bill and David at the cottage
- Bill and David at the Lee Avenue house
- Travel pictures from New York, Cairo, Tangiers, Marrakech, Malaga, Paris, Rome, Montserrat, Amsterdam, London,

Edinburgh, Venice, Berlin, Vienna, Oaxaca, Mexico City, Rio, Buenos Aires, Moscow, St. Petersburg, Kyoto, Tokyo, Vancouver, Whistler, Ottawa, St. John's

- Family pictures with his parents, with my parents, with both sets of parents
- Scenes from the Februaries spent in Puerto Vallarta
- Photos of the Stratford house in its summer glory
- Recent shots of our last home together at the Verve

I return to the living room and alternate between sitting beside his bed and stretching out in the armchair. I try and stay awake because I can't imagine that he can live much longer. He has had no food for over two weeks. He has been unable to take much in the way of fluid for days. This may be his last night.

Chapter Seventeen—Sunday, August 23

The long night dissolves into a pallid dawn. Bill is still breathing.

I decide to have a shower and prepare for the day. As I undress to get into the shower, I suddenly notice that my left foot is purple from heel to toe, the entire foot a deep burgundy. My left leg had been somewhat sore for the past few days, but I was sufficiently distracted with other things going on that I didn't pay much attention. It is sore again this morning and quite significantly swollen in comparison to the right leg.

After a few moments studying the purple foot with curiosity, a dreadful memory surfaces. These symptoms are very similar to those that I experienced in the fall of 2003 after a long flight returning from UN climate change meetings in New Delhi where I had been the coordinator of the World Council of Churches' delegation. I went from the Toronto airport directly to a United Church staff retreat. It was there that I noticed the leg problems. I showed them to Patty, the facilitator for the staff meeting, who also happened to be a trained nurse. She immediately suspected deep-vein thrombosis (DVT)—blood clots. I was rushed to the hospital. An ultrasound was conducted, which confirmed the presence of two blood clots in my left leg. I was given an injection of interferon and placed on a permanent regimen of the blood thinner Coumadin for the rest of my life. Without that intervention by Patty and the subsequent medical treatment, the blood clots could have broken up, sending particles through the blood stream to my lungs or brain. That is how people die of embolisms. I was very lucky.

Now, here I am looking at similar symptoms in the same leg. Based on my previous 2003 experience, I should rush off to an emergency department. But there is a problem. My lover is dying in his hospital bed in our living room. I am convinced we are within hours of his death. I don't want to leave him to die alone while I sit waiting for attention in some hospital.

I can't believe that this is happening.

I need a second opinion. I phone Telehealth Ontario, the provincial hotline for medical advice. I describe my symptoms and my history with DVT. The nurse on the other end of the line recommends that I immediately go to the nearest emergency department.

I weigh the pros and cons of taking or delaying action. What would Bill want me to do? He'd want me to look after myself. But I decide to delay and hope that the blood clots don't break up before tomorrow. I assume that Bill will have died by then, and at that point I can rush off to the hospital.

I become aware that, should I be hit with a fatal embolism, someone is going to have a complicated mess on their hands to sort out. I am not just concerned about the two dead bodies that they would find in our beautiful condo. There would be a myriad of legal and financial matters to sort out. Both Bill's and my wills name the other as the sole beneficiary and executor. Since Bill's diagnosis, I have not had time to get a new will made up. There were more pressing priorities. But if I die now and Bill has died, what happens to our assets?

I sit down at the dining room table and compose the following handwritten note:

August 23, 2009
My partner, William Conklin, is dying of pancreatic cancer.
I, David Hallman, have a history of deep vein thrombosis. From
symptoms presently in my left leg, I believe that I may have another
blood clot.
If I should die, our joint estate should be divided as thus:
... (includes church, charities, and our families)

I list the names and phone numbers for Bill's and my next of kin, our lawyer, and our accountant. I itemise what I can think of as constituting our estate assets and rummage through my files to pull out a few supporting documents.

I place this material on the dining room table on top of the large white binder that contains all the medical notes that have been made on Bill as a client of CCAC over the past two weeks.

Then I shower and shave.

It is 9:00 a.m. The drama of Bill's breathing episodes during the night has abated, and I watch his chest rise and fall in quiet shallow breaths. Sitting at the dining room table drinking my first cup of coffee of the day, I ruminate on the absurdity of the situation and the melodrama of it all. This scene would be considered too far-fetched and not credible were it to be written in a piece of fiction.

I get another thought. John Goodhew, my doctor, had given me his home number years ago in the event that I had some really serious after-hours emergency. I think this might qualify. I call his number.

After a few rings, there is a groggy hello on the other end of the line.

"Hi, John. It's David Hallman. I'm so sorry to be calling you on a Sunday morning. I can tell I'm waking you."

"That's okay. What's up? How's Bill?"

"I'm quite sure that we are in the very final stages. But then again, I have been thinking that he is about to die for the past ten days and he is still here. But actually, it's me I'm calling about."

"What about?"

"I think that I may have another blood clot." I describe the symptoms. "I'm pretty sure that I know you will recommend that I go to emergency, but I don't want to leave Bill right now. I'm prepared to take the risk."

"Tell me, have you been taking your Coumadin?"

"Yes, I have been very disciplined about remembering to take all my meds."

"Well, if you've been taking your Coumadin, and assuming that your INR levels haven't gone all out of whack, it is highly unlikely that what you are experiencing is the result of a blood clot."

"Really? Are you serious?"

"That is the purpose of blood thinners. You don't get blood clots when you are on the blood thinners and if you are taking the appropriate dosage."

"Oh my God. Thank you. What a relief."

"Maybe you've bruised your foot badly. Do you remember banging it on the hospital bed or something?"

"No, nothing that I can recall."

"If you still have these symptoms in the morning and are worried that it might be a clot, I can arrange an emergency ultrasound at a lab near your place."

"Okay. If I need you, I'll give you a call at the office in the morning. Thank you. Thank you. Thank you."

"That's all right. I hope everything goes as well as it can for you and Bill under the circumstances."

I hang up and start thinking about what other explanations there might be. It occurs to me that because I was walking around for the past two weeks without shoes or slippers on so as not to make any noise that might disturb Bill, and since I have spent hours upon hours pacing around the kitchen island using it as my indoor track to help dissipate the stress, perhaps I just really badly bruised the sole of my foot. I put slippers on and stop the pacing.

Over the next several days, the discolouration of my foot fades and the swelling of my leg dissipates.

Bill always referred to Patty, the colleague and nurse who had first diagnosed my DVT in 2003, as my guardian angel. But he didn't leave my health protection exclusively to the kindness of strangers. He was always on my case about overworking and stressing my body and energy too much. Sometimes when I returned totally fatigued from a long trip or a series of meetings at the office, he would complain. "All I get of you is the dregs."

His persistent concern for my health and for the quality of life of our relationship convinced me that my pace of work and the HIV fatigue were killing me. In 1999, I went on part-time disability where I worked 60 percent of the year and had 40 percent time off to rest. That helped somewhat for eight years, but eventually even that amount of part-time work was not sustainable. Bill and my colleagues at the United Church would chide me saying that I was still doing 100 percent of the work only compressing it into 60 percent time. I was burning out fast. In January 2007, I went on full-time permanent disability.

I put the in-case-you-find-me-dead material in a file in the library and come back to the living room to sit beside Bill. I take his hand. His right eye is again partially opened and it seems that he's looking at me. I moisten his dry lips with a swab and tell him about the morning's drama with my faux blood clot. I joke that I thought we were going to be heading off together.

I'm still perplexed by his immobility. He has been in exactly the same pose since Friday morning.

I almost fall off the chair. Maybe ... maybe ... no ... please ... please ... no. I look at his face closely. He's looking back. Oh my God. Don't tell me that he has had a massive stroke. Oh my God. He's paralysed. He's totally fucking paralysed.

I hurry off into the bedroom. I don't want him to see me. I collapse on the bed and bury my head in my hands. All this time, for the past three days, he's been locked inside an ironclad prison. He can't move. He can't signal me. But he's still alive. And I'm convinced he's cognizant. I'm sure of it. He knows what has happened to him and he can't do a thing about it.

My God, his pain was excruciating enough. I didn't think that it could get any worse. Now this. A massive stroke paralysing his whole body. It just got a lot, lot worse.

Bill had been paralysed once before.

We moved into the bungalow on Lee Avenue in the Beach in 1986. Two years later, Bill got the bright idea to make the house work for its keep. Instead of us just forking out money for mortgage payments, taxes, and utility bills, he figured we could turn the house into an income generator, start using it as a bed-and-breakfast.

In no time at all, he had a name ("At-Home-in-the-Beach" which, starting with an "A," meant that it would be near the top in tourist information listings), had signed us up with the Toronto B&B Association, had reconfigured our use of the house (we would rent out all three bedrooms and set up cots for us to sleep on in the curtained-off dining room), had groomed the garden so we could serve breakfast out there daily since we no longer had a usable dining room (our prayers were responsible for the fact that during the summer of 1988 there was not one morning of inclement weather in Toronto), and had started receiving phone calls, bookings, and deposit cheques. He loved the deposit cheques. Even though he refused to travel to the United States because of his political convictions that their government and corporations were responsible for much of the exploitation in the world, he enjoyed receiving the reservation deposits from American tourists. He would tell them that the bank charged him five dollars for each foreign cheque. The bank did no such thing. But he accumulated those five-dollar surcharges and periodically would send them off as a donation to Palestinian relief organisations as his own little gesture to protest American foreign policy. Laurice, my secretary at the United Church at that time, was Palestinian and had come to Canada with her family when their home was confiscated in the late 1940s. She adored Bill and they would have long conversations on the phone.

During the years between 1988 and about 1996, Bill and I figured that between the two of us, we had six jobs. I was working at the United Church, I was managing the renovations at our Stratford house, and I was writing books. Bill was teaching voice and piano lessons, working part-time at an antique store on Queen Street, and managing the B&B business. To say he was managing the B&B is a laughable understatement. He was the B&B. He answered the phone line. He booked the reservations. He handled the record keeping. He did most of the shopping for and preparing of the breakfasts. He cleaned the rooms. He did the laundry. He made up the beds in preparation for the next set of guests.

We had a financial goal to pay off the mortgage on the house. Through the B&B, we were able to meet that goal. But it almost killed Bill.

One morning in 1995 or 1996, he was preparing to make a bed when he suddenly froze. He stood there paralysed. He was so utterly tired that he could not remember how to make it, where the sheets went, what you do with the pillows. Try as he might, his mind had just shut down. He was physically exhausted from the work and mentally exhausted from the stress of always having strangers in our home and always having to be bright and charming when he answered the phone. His immobilisation frightened him. He stopped what he was doing, went downstairs and filled the Jacuzzi with warm water, lit a few candles around the tub, put on soft music, poured himself a cognac, and soaked for an hour.

Once he had recovered, he got on the phone and called me. "Our B&B days are over," he told me. Enough said.

Dianne, the nursing supervisor from Saint Elizabeth's Health Care, comes around noon, substituting again for Meynardo. She's no sooner in the condo than I unload on her about my suspicion that Bill may have had a massive stroke several days ago. She knows that he has been immobile, but she is understandably hesitant to make such a definitive diagnosis. There is nothing that we can do in any case.

She presses me gently again about my fatigue level, encouraging me to reverse my decision not to have anyone stay overnight for relief. I tell her that if Bill is still alive tomorrow, I'll reconsider, but I'd like to be alone with him tonight. I'm convinced he is near the end.

I will be forever grateful that my employer, The United Church of Canada, and John Goodhew, my doctor, supported me in my application to the group insurance provider to go on full-time permanent disability as I did on January 2007. My rationale was that I was pushing myself into an early grave through a combination of the pace of work, the fatigue from the HIV, and the potent antiretroviral drugs that I took to combat it. Going on full-time disability would allow me to rest.

It didn't quite work out that way. As a function of circumstances, I traded one job for another.

My new vocation turned out to be family palliative caregiver. My mother had died about eighteen months earlier and I had spent a lot of time caring for her while she deteriorated in the nursing home. Then, early in 2007, Bill's mom became very ill and I started looking after her until her death in March. Simultaneously, my dad's health was going downhill quickly and I spent much of April camped out in his room in the nursing home, accompanying him as he slowly died. I organised the memorial services for all of our parents and acted as the executor for their estates, filling out the multitudinous forms that governments and insurance companies require on someone's death. Then, in January 2009, my younger brother committed suicide, and I organised two memorial services for him, one in New York and one in our family's hometown of Waterloo. During the late winter and spring of this year, Bill started slipping downhill and I assumed more responsibility for our home life and for his care.

It has all been a lot of work. But it has also been full of blessing. I am immensely privileged to have been able to spend so much time with my parents and with Bill as they went through their final days. These have been the richest experiences of my life. I would not have been able to walk with them so intimately if I had still been working.

I meet Mario in the hall outside our door. I need to prepare him. He and Bill have been good friends, jabbering away in Italian as Bill spent the past few years in his new linguistic endeavour. But I hadn't been able to get through to Mario to tell him about Bill's diagnosis. He had been away from home. Yesterday, he picked up my messages and called me back. Now he is here to visit. And to say good-bye. I tell him that I believe Bill is very near death. Mario is in shock. I take him into the apartment. It is a difficult visit. He holds Bill's hand and sobs. Bill's right eye is open. I detect tears rolling down his cheek.

Over the six months prior to us having our first dance, I watched Bill at the Manatee. He would beckon to a guy and he would push through the crowd to get to Bill. He could get anyone he wanted.

And he chose me.

The sun has set. The music is playing softly. A candle is burning beside his Jesus picture.

I go into the bedroom to lie down for a little nap.

I wake up with a start. I don't know what woke me.

The clock on my night table says 10:20 p.m.

I get up and walk into the living room to check on Bill. I sit down in the chair beside the bed and take his hand.

The shallow, quiet breathing that had been the norm today shifts into high gear. He starts breathing deeply and audibly. I tighten my grip. I think his right eye is slightly open, but I can't tell for sure.

One last time I say, "Good-bye, my darling. I love you."

More deep, loud, breaths for about five minutes.

Then it stops.

I wait and wait and wait.

He's gone.

Thank God. It's over.

Thank God. He is out of pain.

Thank God. He's at peace.

Epilogue

Photo Album

1959 – Bill as a teenager. High school picture.

1977 – Bill in our first condo, Massey Square, Toronto.

1979 – Spain. Bill at Benedictine Abbey of Montserrat that we visited
while on a trip to Barcelona to pay homage to Gaudi and Miró.

1980 – Egypt. In front of the Great Sphinx of Giza during our
trip that included Cairo, Luxor and the Valley of the Kings.

1986 – Cottage life. Cross-country skiing at our
cottage in the Kawartha Lakes District.

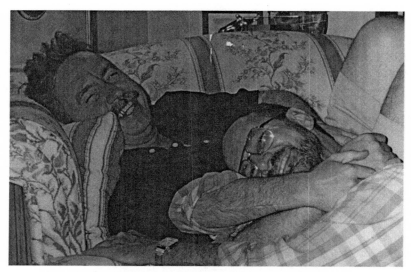

1989 – In our Lee Avenue home in Toronto where we ran a bed-and-breakfast. We figured that at the time, we were working at six jobs between the two of us. No wonder we were tired.

1990 – Mexico. Bill in conversation with a potter in Oaxaca. Bill was also a potter and created beautiful art pieces.

1991 – Morocco. Bill in the souk (market) in Tangier.

1994 – On top of Blackcomb Mountain at Whistler, BC.

1995 – France. On the Japanese Bridge over the water
lilies pond at Monet's home in Giverny.

1997 – Japan. Tea ceremony in Kyoto when Bill joined
me after I had finished my work at the UN Climate
Summit that adopted the Kyoto Protocol.

1999 – Italy. In front of *Don Giovanni* poster at La Scala
in Milan. Of course, we dressed more formally in the
evening for the performance. This was Italy after all.

1999 – Italy. In Piazza San Marco, Venice. So romantic.

2000 – France. At Trocadero with view of the Eiffel Tower. Bill had studied at the Sorbonne in Paris for two years in the late 1960s and I spent a year studying there in the early 1970s. When we met in 1976 and discovered that we had both studied in Paris, we took that as a sign that we were meant to be together.

2001 – Bill's Toast to Life.
I used this picture for Bill's memorial service.

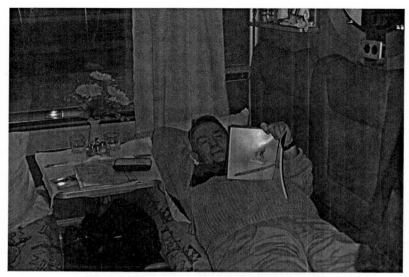

2003 – Russia. Bill in our cabin on the Aurora Express
train from Moscow to St. Petersburg. He's holding a book
from a Fabergé exhibition we had just visited.

2003 – The last outing with our parents to the Stratford
Festival for a performance of *The King and I.*

2004 – Mexico. Together at Casa de los Arcos in Puerto
Vallarta where we stayed every February for many years.

2006 – At the Museum of Civilization across the river from
the Canadian Parliament Buildings in Ottawa during a quiet
trip that we took to celebrate our 30th anniversary.

2007 – A summer lunch on the veranda of our Stratford house.

2007 – Our Stratford house had been built in 1877 and
was in a dilapidated state when we bought it in 1991. Bill
restored it to its former glory as this 2007 photo shows.

2007 – In front of a portrait of Bill's mother Adelle
during the remembrance celebration that we held in
our Stratford house following her death.

2009 – The living room of the Verve condo, our final
home together. We set up the hospital bed in this room so
that Bill could be near his piano and see the view.

2009 – Toronto skyline as seen from our Verve condo. The view that Bill would see from his hospital bed in the living room.

E-mail Announcement Sent August 23, 2009 11:30 p.m.

Dear family and friends,

William Conklin, our Billy-boy, is gone, his spirit free of the body that had become an excruciating prison.

He was a beloved family member to some of you, a devoted friend to others of you. To me, he was my loving partner for thirty-three years. Some of you met him in that capacity, my better half.

Bill died quietly on Sunday evening, August 23, 2009, with me by his side in our Toronto home. Bill's death was as a result of rapid onset pancreatic cancer, which had spread to the liver, lungs, and abdominal lymph nodes. It was diagnosed on Friday, August 7. His physical decline accelerated very quickly over the subsequent two weeks.

During his final two weeks, he felt enveloped by Jesus's embrace. He was ready and indeed anxious to go. He knew that he was loved by God and wanted all of us to know that we are as well.

We are immeasurably blessed for having had him in our lives. His spirit will continue to enrich us all our days.

Love, David

P.S. He told me to say good-bye to you, and he sends his love.

P.P.S. Visitation—Saturday, September 12, 2–4 p.m. and 7–9 p.m. at Rosar-Morrison Funeral Home, 467 Sherbourne Street, Toronto, ON, M4X 1K5. Tel. (416) 924-1408, www.rosar-morrison.com. Memorial Service—St. Luke's United Church, 353 Sherbourne Street, Toronto on Sunday, September 13 at 2:00 p.m. Reception to follow.

**You are invited to
an Early Christmas**

Suite 3109 at the Verve

**Tuesday, September 1
7:00 to 9:00 p.m.**

As an expression of appreciation for the wonderful support in thought, word, and deed that you provided to Bill and me during the past few weeks, I would like to invite you to drop by for a glass of wine in Bill's honour and to pick out one of our Christmas decorations that we had decided to give away to our friends as a little tangible reminder for you of Bill.

Love, David

A Celebration of the Life of
William Conklin
Sunday, September 13, 2009
2:00 p.m.
Saint Luke's United Church
353 Sherbourne Street, Toronto

At time of gathering: recorded musical selections of some of Bill and David's favourite pieces, composers, and artists.

Prelude—"Ach Gott, erhör mein Seufzen und Weh Klagen" (O God, Mark Thou My Sighs and All My Anguish) by J. T. Krebs performed by Boris Treivus

Welcome—Rev. Hoon Kim

Prayer of Approach—Rev. Gordon Winch

Hymn—*Breathe on Me, Breath of God*, V.U. #382

Scripture and Meditation—Rev. Dr. Rob Oliphant and David Hallman, based on John 15:15

Music—"He Has Gone" by Oscar Peterson performed by Boris Treivus

Readings

- Excerpt from Dante's *The Divine Comedy Vol. 3: Paradise*, read by Marco Fiola
- Selected limericks from Edward Lear's *Book of Nonsense*, read by Maureen Argon and Brendan Howley
- "Go Down Death" from *God's Trombones* by James Weldon Johnson, performed by Walter Borden

Music—"Hear My Song" by Jason Robert Brown, performed by David Ambrose, Darryl Burton, Shannon Butcher, Sabrina Santelli, Zandée Toovey, and Boris Treivus

The Bill I Knew and Loved

- Doug O'Neill
- Huda Abbasi
- Laurice Mahli and William MacKinnon
- Peter Spencer and Eric Marshall
- Tamara Glazier
- Denny Young

Music—"But Beautiful" by Jimmy Van Heusen/Johnny Burke, performed by Elaine Overholt

Prayer—Rev. Malcolm Finlay

The 23rd Psalm (recited in unison)—Rev. Hoon Kim

The Lord is my shepherd, I shall not want.
He makes me lie down in green pastures;
he leads me beside still waters;
he restores my soul.
He leads me in the paths of righteousness
for his name's sake.
Even though I walk through the darkest valley,
I fear no evil;
for you are with me;
your rod and your staff—they comfort me.
You prepare a table before me in the presence of my enemies;
you anoint my head with oil; my cup overflows.
Surely goodness and mercy shall follow me
all the days of my life,
and I shall dwell in the house of the Lord forever.

Music—Ashley MacIsaac

Dedication—Rev. Hoon Kim

Blessing and Benediction—Rev. Hoon Kim

Postlude—"Christ Lag in Todesbanden" (Christ lay in death's bonds) by J. S. Bach, performed by Boris Treivus

At time of departing: recorded musical selections of some of Bill and David's favourite pieces, composers, and artists.

Reception in Parlour and Friendship Room

Thank God for Good Friends

Theological reflection prepared by David Hallman
and read during service on David's behalf by Rob Oliphant
Sunday, September 13, 2009
Saint Luke's United Church, Toronto

"And Jesus said ... I call you friend ..." John 15:15

Four days before we got the diagnosis of pancreatic cancer, the L. L. Bean catalogue arrived in our mail box. Bill liked the classy yet rugged look of the clothing lines carried by L. L. Bean. He devoured each page of the catalogue and in no time had picked out several shirts that he wanted. After all the weight he had lost over the previous months, he was proud of his new svelte figure and determined to have a smart new wardrobe for the fall. He asked me to phone the 1-800 number and place the order. I was happy to do so because I knew this would make him happy. After all, what are friends for?

We both knew that he was sick. We didn't know how sick. But at that point, prediagnosis, Bill wasn't thinking about dying. He was thinking about looking dashing. Or maybe he was thinking about dying and with his characteristic obstinacy was determined to be the first in history to defy the adage "you can't take it with you."

We have been friends a long time. Our thirty-third anniversary occurred on August 17, while he lay increasingly incapacitated in a hospital bed in our living room.

In days gone by, those of us in a certain community used to say, when introducing our partners, "He's my 'friend.'" The implied quotation marks around "friend" were indicated by a raised eyebrow, a wink, or a nudge. It signified that this person was a lot more than a mere acquaintance.

159

I've been thinking a lot over the past few weeks about what it means to be a friend. And my reflections were prompted by two incidents with Bill on the day we got his diagnosis.

At around 5:30 p.m. on Friday, August 7, we were sitting in a room at Toronto East General Hospital waiting for the doctor to return with the results of the tests that they had conducted during the day. Bill was in a bed and I was sitting beside him. We were holding hands. In walked the doctor, looking grim. In a sensitive yet professional manner, she said, "I have the results of the tests, particularly the CAT scan, and I am very sorry to have to tell you that it is very bad news." She then described the virulence and pervasiveness of the cancer indicated by the tests.

Bill looked at me and in a calm voice said, "Are you alright?"

"Noooooooooooooooooo," I cried. Thinking back, I was in shock, but he was calm and, as the best of friends, his immediate reaction was one of concern for me.

We drove home in silence. We had already agreed that whatever the results, we wanted to have him cared for at home. Once we got back up into the apartment, he went to bed to rest as I convulsed on the living room floor, trying to stifle any sound so as not to disturb him.

About an hour later, he awoke laughing. Not a little giggle but hearty robust laughter. I ran into the bedroom. Bill's eyes were radiant. He described a dream that he had just had walking in the garden with Jesus, who had just called him his best friend. They had laughed together and kibitzed. Jesus had even told him that he was looking sexy. Bill loved that. Jesus also told him that he should drop any burdens that he was carrying, forget any of the things for which he felt guilty. All was forgiven. He was loved and Jesus was ready to welcome him into heaven. His pain would soon be over.

My prayers of the past few months had been answered. My most fervent prayers had been that Bill would experience spiritual peace. Spiritual peace he now had in spades!

For the next few days, our conversations and our prayers were of thanksgiving— for the wonderful life we had had together, for the wonderful experiences that we had had, for the wonderful friendships with which we had been blessed, for the vibrant communities of which we had been a part.

Later, our prayers did turn more toward petition because, though Bill's spirit was ready and anxious to leave, his body would not set it free. The pain and the distress worsened. We prayed that it would be over soon. After about two weeks, on Sunday evening, August 23, quietly and with me by his side holding his hand, my friend breathed his last.

In John 15:15, we read that Jesus said "... I call you friend ..." The thrust of Jesus's message was that he was signalling a new relationship with his disciples, one of equality between him and them. What is the implication for us? We are to love each other as Jesus loves us. As a good friend.

Bill specified only one thing that he wanted to make sure I would say at his memorial service. He asked me to tell his family members and his friends this simple injunction: "Be kind to each other." That's what he wants of us. To be kind to each other.

That is one of the key ingredients in being a good friend.

Jesus called Bill his friend. And now he has also called this friend away from us and into his arms.

Thank God for good friends.

William V. Conklin

Bill Conklin died at home in Toronto with his longtime partner
David Hallman by his side on
Sunday, August 23, 2009.
Cause of death was rapid onset pancreatic cancer diagnosed on
Friday, August 7, 2009.
He was predeceased by his parents, William Joseph and Adelle Mary
(née Bennett). He is survived by his partner David, aunts Connie,
June, Lenna, Marion, Mary, and Muriel and numerous cousins.
Bill lived life to the fullest every day in his music teaching, his
pottery and painting, his nurturing of children and persons in
distress, his love of languages, his passion for the arts, his wide
circle of friends, his enjoyment of a good party, the travels to many
parts of the world that he and David took, decorating the homes
in which they lived, his advocacy for social and ecological justice,
and his practical actions to help people and the earth.
Bill will be profoundly missed by David, members of both Bill's
and David's families, many friends in Toronto, Stratford, and
Puerto Vallarta, and by generations of music students.
On the wall in the garden room of their home in Stratford, Bill
painted the following Latin motto
Dum vivimos, vivamos,
which translated means
While we are alive, let's really live!

Jesus said, I have called you friend … (John 15:15)

Appreciations

David is grateful for the participation of all those who provided leadership in this memorial service.

David would also like to express his profound appreciation to the many organisations and individuals for the support that they gave, which made it possible for Bill to be cared for at home during his severe illness right until the end:

- Toronto East General Hospital
- Community Care Access Centre (Toronto Central)
- Saint Elizabeth Health Care
- Toronto Homemaking Service
- Temmy Latner Centre for Palliative Care, Mt. Sinai Hospital
- Board, property manager, and staff of the Verve, which has been home for Bill and David since October 2008
- Saint Luke's United Church staff and congregation
- Rosar-Morrison Funeral Home
- Many, many friends, neighbours, and family members who provided invaluable emotional support, practical assistance, and unstinting love.

Recorded Musical Selections
Favourites of Bill and David

1. "Pie Jesu" (Gentle Jesus) from *Requiem* by Gabriel Fauré. Sung by Kiri te Kanawa.
2. "The Prayer" by D. Foster/C. Bayer Sager. Sung by RyanDan.
3. "Caro mio ben" (My dear beloved) by Giuseppe Giordani. Sung by Cecilia Bartoli.
4. "I Remember You" by J. Mercer/V. Schertzinger. Sung by Dinah Washington.
5. "Non mi dir, bell'idol mio" (Do not tell me, my true love) from *Don Giovanni* by Amadeus Mozart. Sung by Joan Sutherland
6. "Barcelona" by Freddie Mercury/Mike Moran. Sung by Freddie Mercury and Montserrat Caballé.
7. "O Sacred Head Sore Wounded" from *St. Matthew Passion* by Bach. Sung by the Münchener Bach-Chor.
8. "Our Love Is Here to Stay" by I. Gershwin/G. Gershwin. Sung by Natalie Cole.
9. "Lascia ch'io pianga" (Let me weep) from *Rinaldo* by G. F. Handel. Sung by Cecilia Bartoli.
10. "Time to Say Goodbye" by F. Sartori/L. Quarantotta. Sung by Andrea Bocelli and Sarah Brightman.
11. "Nessun dorma" (No one must sleep) from *Manon Lescaut* by G. Puccini. Sung by Ben Heppner.
12. "Someone to Watch Over Me" by I. Gershwin/ G. Gershwin. Sung by Keely Smith.
13. "Behold the Lamb of God" from *The Messiah* by G. F. Handel. Sung by the Toronto Mendelssohn Choir.

14. "Don't Cry Baby" by S. Unger/S. Bernie/J. Johnson. Sung by Etta James.
15. "D'amor sull'ali rosee" (On the rosy wings of love) from *Il Trovatore* by Verdi. Sung by Leontyne Price.
16. "Charmed Life" by Diana Krall. Sung by Diana Krall.
17. "Morgen" (Tomorrow) by Richard Straus. Sung by Jessye Norman.
18. "I'll Be There" by H. David/B. Gordy Jr./W. Hutch/B. West. Sung by RyanDan.
19. "Aria" and "Variation 1"—*Goldberg Variations* by J. S. Bach. Performed by Glenn Gould.
20. "Unforgettable" by I. Gordon. Sung by Nat King Cole and Natalie Cole.

Good-bye, my love
Service of Interment
November 23, 2009
Avondale Cemetery, Stratford

Dear Bill,

Though in some ways you will always be with me, today is a particularly profound moment of saying good-bye. There is a symbolic finality to this ritual of placing your ashes and these roses in our niche. As I do so, these are words that I want to say to you, the love of my life.

I am thankful for how vivaciously we shared our lives together. We sparked each other. We inspired the best in each other. We were never bored.

I am thankful for your big heart, for the ways in which you welcomed family, friends, and strangers into our home, for your capacity to reach out to someone in need, masking your own physical fatigue behind sparkling eyes and a robust smile.

I am thankful for how passionate we both were about the arts. We enjoyed performances in every major opera house and exhibits in every major museum around the world. We debated books, plays, and films. We always had music in our home. Among my most treasured memories are the times of our duets, you singing Giordani or Schubert while I accompanied you on the piano.

I am thankful for how you made me laugh and how you made so many other people laugh.

I am thankful for the beautiful environments you created in our homes with your design skill, artistic taste, and appreciation for the ancient and the modern.

I am thankful for your sense of adventure as we travelled together to distant lands and from coast to coast in Canada. I am just sorry that we were not able to realise two of your remaining dreams—to spend a year studying art and Italian in Venice and to dance on the Great Wall of China.

I am thankful for the ways we learned from each other and supported each other in trying to make the world a better place.

I am thankful for how we teamed together in caring for our parents as they aged. We gave them shelter, hosted them at our dinner table, and provided comfort in times of distress.

I am thankful for the depth of faith that we shared. We came from different religious traditions and we sometimes varied in our theological understandings. But Christian faith was essential to both of us, not only in what we believed but in how we practiced it in the world. Having these shared spiritual values enriched beyond measure our thirty-three-year union and made a sacred time of how we faced together your dying days.

I am thankful for the way that you cared for me. I am still alive and thriving today because of your concern for my health, your insistence that I curb my debilitating pace of work life, and your support during times of physical and emotional trial.

I am thankful that you let me care for you. Your last months and particularly your final two weeks were excruciatingly painful for you and numbingly arduous for me. But we lived them together, side by side. Being able to care for you in our home for those final days was the last great gift of love that I could give to you. Letting me give you that gift was your last great act of generosity to me.

I am thankful for your spirit of impatience and irreverence. You abhorred the maudlin and you now think this good-bye message is going on too long. I hear you saying "Enough, already!"

So, good-bye, my love. Rest well. Your time of peace has come.

Love, David

CPSIA information can be obtained at www.ICGtesting.com
Printed in the USA
LVOW080648020713

341032LV00001B/11/P